Calico Country Crafts

Books by Leslie Linsley

The Weekend Quilt
The Great American Quilt Banner
First Steps In Counted Cross Stitch
First Steps in Stenciling
First Steps in Quilting
Carry-Along Crochet
Country Decorating with Fabric Crafts
Leslie Linsley's Night Before Christmas Craft Book
Leslie Linsley's Christmas Ornaments and Stockings
America's Favorite Quilts
Million Dollar Projects from the 5 & 10¢ Store
Making It Personal With Monograms, Initials and Names
The Great Bazaar
Army/Navy Surplus: A Decorating Source
Afghans to Knit and Crochet
Quick and Easy Knit and Crochet
Custom Made
Wildcrafts
The Decoupage Workshop
Decoupage: A New Look at an Old Craft
Decoupage for Young Crafters
Air Crafts
Fabulous Furniture Decorations
New Ideas for Old Furniture
Photocrafts
Scrimshaw

Calico Country Crafts

by
Leslie Linsley

St. Martin's Press
New York

Preparation and Design: Jon Aron Studio

Project Director: Robby Smith
Illustrations: Peter Peluso, Jr.
Photography: Jon Aron
Crafters: Ruth Linsley
Helen Jenkins
Kate Ciffone
Susan Fernald Joyce

Library of Congress Cataloging-in-Publication Data

Linsley, Leslie.
    Calico country crafts.

    1. Calico craft.   I. Title.
TT699.L55   1988   746'.0421   87-43319
ISBN 0-312-00867-8

10 9 8 7 6 5 4 3 2

Acknowledgments

I am especially grateful to the manufacturers who have been helpful in the preparation of this book. Their cooperation and interest in the project have been most generous. They are:

Fairfield Processing Corporation, Danbury, Connecticut

Laura Ashley, Inc., New York, New York

V.I.P. Fabrics, a division of Cranston Print Works Company, New York, New York

Contents

Calico Country Crafts

Introduction

Every time I pick up a magazine I wonder if our interest in country decorating will ever disappear. It's hard to believe that we were ever unaware of its existence, since we've been exposed to country style and country folk crafts all our lives.

Every time I hear the word *calico* it evokes a country scene. Home crafters have long been familiar with calico cotton prints, which have always been used for making toys, bed coverings, wallhangings, and clothing.

Because of the extraordinary range of colors and the small, overall patterns, it is easy to design, mix, and match these wonderful fabrics. Usually made of 100 percent cotton, calico has always been a favorite with quilt makers. Once a quilt is made, there follows a basketful of calico scraps. Since calico is inexpensive and widely available, it is used for more crafting projects than any other fabric. Whether you are crafting for a contemporary, traditional, or country environment, there is a calico that can be used. For all these reasons calico has remained with us and has become synonymous with country crafts.

Most of the projects shown here do not require more than a yard or two, and in most cases scraps, quarter yards, and half yards are all you'll need. Scraps of fabric can be used to make surprisingly varied and interesting craft projects. Add warmth to any room with a calico patchwork quilt. A wallhanging softens an area and a patchwork tablecloth expresses a feeling of coziness. No matter how modern a room, the addition of a quilted pillow in the corner of a couch gives the room character. It says, "The people who live here enjoy their environment," and it is instantly inviting.

It's always nicer to give a handmade gift than one that has been purchased. In this way the item can be personalized with colors, fabric, texture, and design to suit the person you will give it to. Made with scraps and love, the gift projects cost pennies and will add to your crafting enjoyment.

For a real country Christmas, calico ornaments, decorations, and stockings are a natural. This is the time to get out all the odds and ends of ribbons, sequins, buttons, and trimmings and have some fun. You'll be surprised to find the newest calico Christmas patterns in up-to-the-minute designs. You'll find bright and bold reds and greens as well as country berry and sage that go well with nature's vines, pinecones, and evergreens.

Use all the tiniest leftover fabrics to make no-cost bazaar best-sellers. This is the time to be most creative and use up the last bit of scraps for an extra special fund-raiser. The projects can be made in quantity as well and even make good gifts.

My favorite projects are anything to make for babies. V.I.P. Fabrics, a division of Cranston Print Works Company, has a line of fabrics called V.I.B.—Very Important Bears. They come in all the right colors for a bright and bold or pastel-soft baby's room, or for making a delightful patchwork jacket, and much more. You'll be able to make coordinated quilts, pillows, mobiles, wallhangings, and all the wonderful accessories for a child's room. It is so easy or, as I like to say, "sew-easy," and affordable. The patchwork teddy bear is fun to make and to give just to see your favorite child's eyes light up at the sight of it.

Whether you decide to make one project to give as a gift or decorate your entire house with calico, you can't miss. The finished results will have that ever winning country charm.

Happy crafting!

LL

General Crafting How-To's

Each time I write a book (I've written more than thirty), I try to imagine what suggestions, tips, and information would be helpful for crafting in general, and generally applicable to the various projects in the book. I know that many of you are beginners, new to crafting, as well as experienced craftworkers seeking new ideas and designs. My mail is filled with questions, suggestions, thank yous, and admonitions for my omissions. I am truly grateful to all of you who take the time to write, even though it sometimes takes me weeks, even months, to respond. It is through your interest that I can attempt to get better, to give you more complete information.

Designing projects and writing directions for others to make them has been my career for over twenty years. Over the years the variety of materials for each craft has expanded and techniques for making things better and more easily have improved. It is especially challenging when I am asked to track down a product for a specific use. Along the way I usually uncover a few new ones that I might not have been aware of.

The following are tried and true basic crafting techniques that apply to many of the projects here, as well as supplies, tools, and tips on how to do things better, more quickly and easily, and at less expense. Skim through these pages before you begin the projects and refer back to them when necessary. The bold headings make it easy to locate specific information. And if you have some ideas to share, I'm always happy to hear from you.

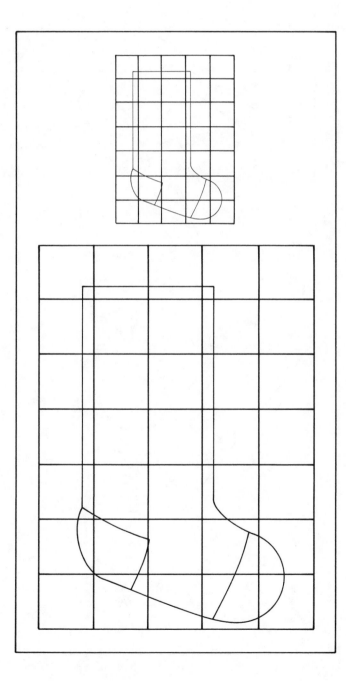

Enlarging Designs and Patterns

Most of the patterns and designs are presented full size. Occasionally, however, it is necessary to enlarge a design. In this case you will find a grid over the design, with an indication of the size each square represents. Usually one square equals 1 inch. You then transfer the design to, or copy it onto, paper marked off into 1-inch squares. You can make your own graph paper or buy a pad in an art supply store.

Copying Designs

Place a piece of tracing paper over the design or pattern and copy each line with a marker, pen, or pencil. You can use this paper pattern to cut out the fabric pieces by pinning it directly onto the chosen fabric and cutting around the drawn lines. All pattern pieces are given with a ¼-inch seam allowance, unless otherwise stated.

Transferring Designs and Patterns

You can transfer most of the designs from this book to your fabric. Simply trace the design on a sheet of tracing paper, then retrace the design on the back of the tracing paper. Place the paper over the fabric and rub a pencil over the outlines of the design. Remove the tracing and go over the design so you can see it more clearly on the fabric.

Another method is to place a piece of dressmaker's tracing (carbon) paper on the right side of the fabric, carbon side down, with traced design on top. Go over all pattern lines with a tracing wheel or ballpoint pen to transfer the design. Remove the carbon and tracing.

Transferring Design Details

After you've traced and transferred the outline of a pattern or design, you will have to mark the fabric for any details, such as the eyes of a cat or the placement of buttons on a jacket.

To do this, place the pattern on the right side of the fabric. Using a sharp soft-lead pencil, poke a hole through the tracing to mark the fabric. When you are marking for an overlay of one fabric on another, as with the wing of the duck on page 83, make evenly spaced dots around the outline of the wing, in this case, and remove the paper. Then connect the dots. If you are using a dark fabric you'll need white chalk to mark your lines.

Another method that I often use is to tape my traced design onto a window pane with the fabric taped over it. The design will show through light fabrics or light colors and you then simply trace the outline of the pattern onto the fabric with a soft pencil, or with a washable pen (see Sources for Supplies, page 175).

Making a Template

A template is a pattern that is rigid and full size. It can be cut from cardboard or plastic acetate. Some templates used for quilting are made from sandpaper because it is the acceptable weight and won't slip on the fabric. I prefer the oak tag used for manila folders. It is inexpensive and easy to cut.

A template is used to trace the design elements when you are making more than one and can't use the paper pattern. It is also used to make appliqués. Transfer the pattern to the template material by first tracing the design. Place the tracing face down on the oak tag and rub over each traced line. For a sharper image, place a piece of carbon paper on the oak tag with the tracing on top. Go over each line with a pencil. Remove the tracing and cut out the design outline using a sharp scissors (not the pair used for fabric). All patterns in this book that call for a template include a ¼-inch seam allowance. In this way you will place the template on the fabric, draw around it as many times as required for the number of pieces needed, and then cut the fabric out along the drawn lines.

Cutting Out Patterns

Take the time to determine how you will place each pattern piece on the fabric to get the most from your material. When cutting out the front and back of a pattern such as one of the animal pillows on page 76, remember to cut one from the front of the fabric and one with the fabric turned to the wrong side, or cut one pattern piece from the folded fabric so you end up with two pieces in the correct positions.

Sewing

Sewing pattern pieces in the right sequence makes a big difference in time and efficiency, as well as accuracy.

Plan thread colors so that, where possible, all stitching with one color can be done before

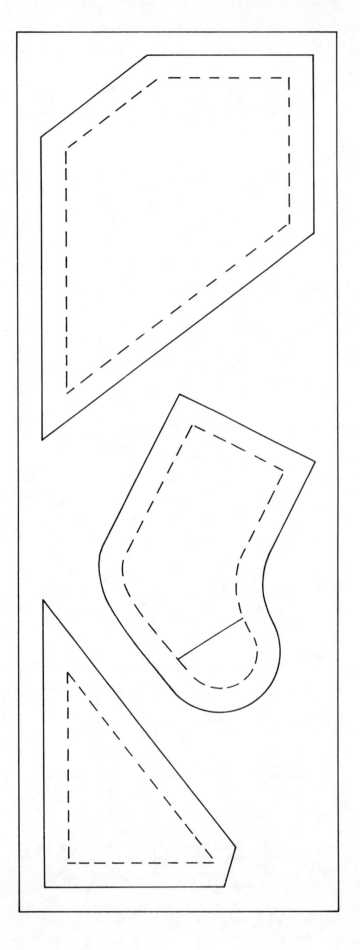

changing spool and bobbin. If you're working in quantity (making a batch of ornaments or projects to sell at a bazaar, for example) do each step on every piece before going on, rather than completing one and starting the next.

Any hand or lap work, such as stuffing and finishing openings, should be done at one time. I like to save these finishing details to do while relaxing.

If you're making patchwork fabric, as I did for the teddy bear on page 94, plan the arrangement of the squares so you don't end up with all of one print together. You want the overall effect to be varied as well as harmonious.

Sewing Points: Many traditional quilting patterns are created from triangles, diamonds, and similar shapes. The points made by the joining of these shapes present a challenge and require special care. The star pattern for the tablecloth on page 54 is one that requires this attention.

When stitching two pieces together, sew along the stitch line, but do not sew into the seam allowance at each point. It helps to mark the finished points with a pin so you can begin and end your seams at these marks.

Inward Corner Edge: Place a pin across the point of the stiches and clip up to the stitches in the seam allowance in order to turn the fabric under.

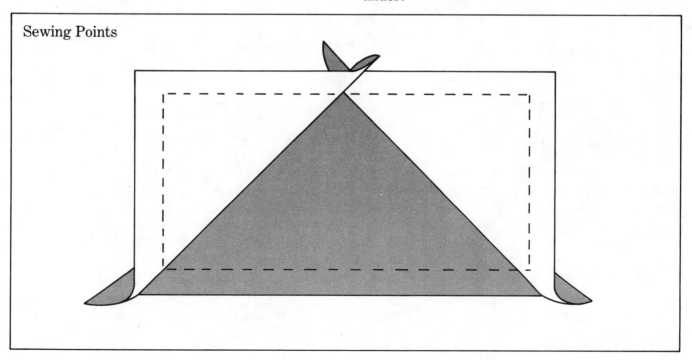

Sewing Points

Outward Corner Edge: Once you've stitched around a corner, clip off half the seam allowance across the point. Turn the fabric back, press the seams open, and trim the excess fabric away.

Turning Corners: It's often a bit difficult to turn corners and continue a seam line. Figure 1 shows the three pieces to be joined. With right sides facing, stitch piece A to piece B as in Figure 2. Next, join C to A as in Figure 3. Leave the needle down in the fabric. Lift the presser foot and using point of scissors, clip the seam to the needle. Slide B under C and adjust so the edges of B align with C. Lower the presser foot and stitch along the seam line.

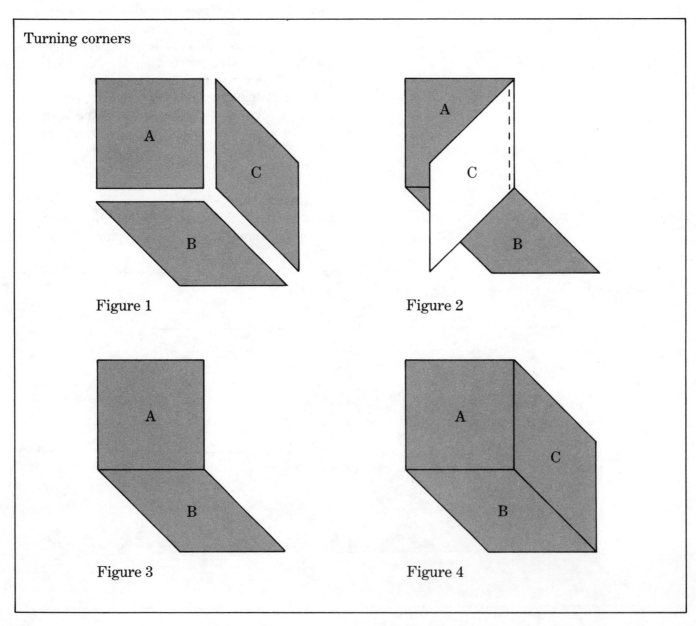

Turning corners

Figure 1

Figure 2

Figure 3

Figure 4

Quilting

Quilting is the means by which you sew layers of fabric and batting together to produce a padded fabric held together by stitching. It is warm and decorative and is generally the finishing step in appliqué and patchwork projects.

You can quilt all the fabrics used for the projects here, making them appear three-dimensional and giving a sculpted effect. The quilting is what makes a project interesting and gives it a textured look.

Hand Quilting: The favored technique among seasoned quilters is hand quilting. While most of the piecing for the top of a quilt is done on the machine, the actual quilting is done by hand. This is what makes a quilt so appealing and authentic-looking.

The most comfortable way to quilt is over a frame or in a large hoop, which keeps the fabric taut and allows you to make even stitches. Before quilting you will baste and mark the fabric.

Give the knotted end of your thread a good tug and pull it through the backing fabric into the batting and through the top. Keep your thread fairly short and take small running stitches. Follow your premarked quilting lines.

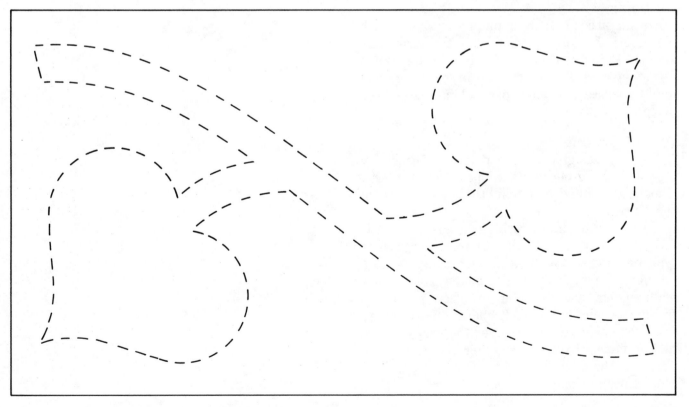

Machine Quilting: This is easier, quicker, and often preferred for small projects such as placemats, Christmas ornaments, sachets, etc. Use thin quilt batting for machine stitching and set the stitch length for a looser stitch, such as nine stitches per inch.

Marking Patterns for Quilting: Before basting the top, batting, and back of the quilt fabric together, mark the quilting design on the top of the fabric. Spread the top on a hard, flat surface to transfer your design.

Use a light pencil or a water-soluble pen to mark the pattern. Once all the quilting is complete, the lines that are visible can be removed with a squirt bottle. For dark fabrics, use a piece of chalk or dressmaker's marker. Use a template when possible to mark your patterns. A yardstick is good for diagonal lines. Mark on the fabric along both edges of the yardstick, then flip it over and continue to mark along the edge for perfectly spaced quilting lines.

Basting: Before quilting, baste the top fabric, batting, and backing together. Begin at the center and take long, loose stitches outward. These stitches will be cut away after all quilting has been completed.

Outlining

To emphasize each appliqué or patchwork piece, stitch along each side of the seam line about a ¼ inch on the outside and inside. When using an overall grid fabric, for example, you might want to quilt along parallel lines across the design.

Overall Quilting

Quilting designs are the patterns formed by stitches on the borders and open area of fabric. Choose a simple design to fill these large areas of the fabric.

Circles, grids, and swirling feathers, as well as hearts, diamonds, and squares are often used as quilting designs. When a quilted design is used on the borders of a quilt or around a tablecloth or wallhanging, for example, it often serves to frame the center design. Elaborate patterns are found on early quilts and, over the years, give a quilted fabric character. Due to repeated use and washing, the fabric fades and sometimes puckers to accentuate the quilting.

Right Triangles

There is a quick and easy way to join light and dark triangles to create squares of any size. You can use this method to make a patchwork project when lots of two-color triangles are needed to make up the variety of squares.

Determine the size of your finished unit, then add 1 inch to it. For example, if you want to create 2-inch squares, use a yardstick to draw a grid of 3-inch squares on the wrong side of your fabric.

Next, draw a diagonal line through all squares as shown in the diagram. Pin marked fabric to a piece of another fabric the same size, with right sides facing. Stitch a ¼-inch seam on each side of the drawn diagonal lines as shown.

Cut on all solid lines to get the individual units of light and dark, or contrasting fabric triangles. Clip the corners, open, and press.

Strip Piecing

This is the method by which you sew strips of different fabrics together and then cut them into units that are arranged to make up the entire quilt or pillow top. Rather than cutting and sewing individual squares together over and over again, two or more strips of fabric are sewn to-

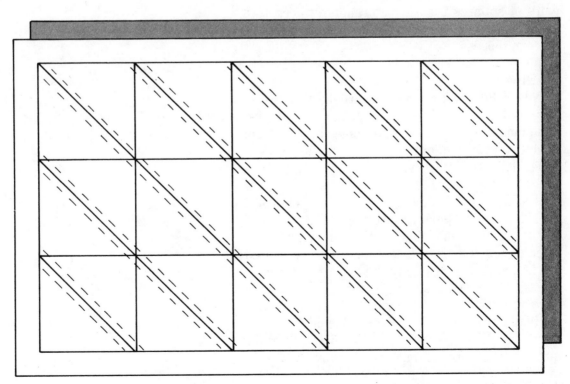

Right triangle method

gether and then cut into segments that are of the exact same dimensions. These units are then arranged and stitched together in different positions to form the quilt pattern.

Making Patchwork Fabric

Often it's fun to take small, 1½- or 2-inch squares and sew them together at random to create your own patchwork fabric. In this way you can choose the color combination, wash and fade it to look old, and use it to cut out small pattern pieces. I used this method for making heart-shaped sachets and on page 150 for the patchwork teddy bear. Combine colors with muslin; use pastels with a bright color like red thrown in only now and then.

Use a yardstick to mark a grid on the back of a variety of fabric pieces. Cut out all squares. Remember to add a ¼-inch seam allowance. Pair a muslin square with a printed square and with right sides facing sew a batch together in the following way: Line up one edge of two squares and stitch on the machine, do not cut thread. Continue to run the machine for a couple of stitches and then join the next pair of squares. Keep stitching squares of fabric together in this way so you have a chain of attached squares. Cut them apart, open seams, and press. Next join pairs of squares together at random to create a larger piece of fabric from which you can cut your pattern pieces.

Stuffing

Poly-Fil™ stuffing from Fairfield Processing Corporation is used to stuff all the toys, pillows, and small quilted projects. It comes in bags from which you can pull out small amounts as needed. When it is necessary to fill small areas, such as the ears of a teddy bear or the points of a Christmas star, I use a crochet hook or the end of a broken pencil to push the stuffing into place.

For quilts, you'll find batting in a variety of thicknesses and sizes. The information is printed on the bag, so you can buy the exact size for your needs. The pillows shown in the book are standard size and can be filled with a pillow form, also available from Fairfield Processing and sold at fabric shops. Save small pieces of batting for quilting the tops of pillows and toys or ornaments.

Hand Stitching

Some of the projects suggest embroidered stitches for the finishing touches. The stuffed projects are closed with a slip stitch, which is invisible. The following stitches are the most commonly used:

Basic Stitches

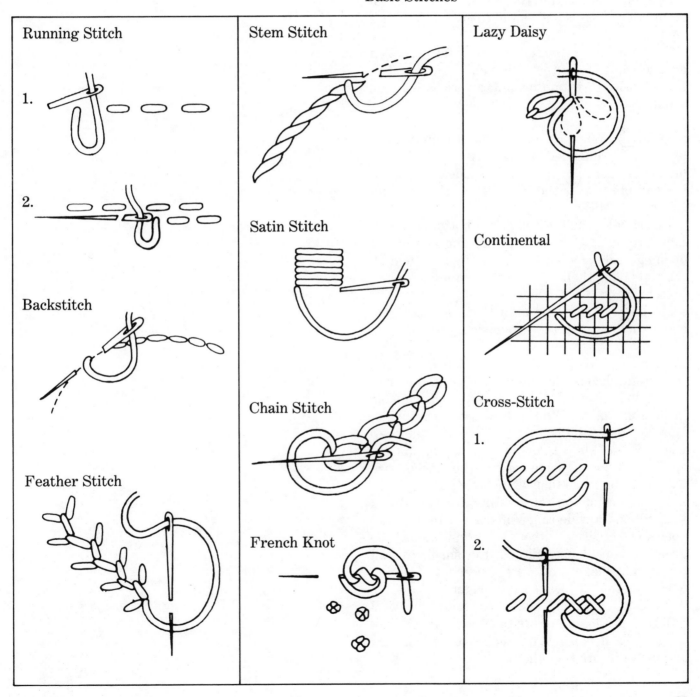

Running Stitch

1.

2.

Backstitch

Feather Stitch

Stem Stitch

Satin Stitch

Chain Stitch

French Knot

Lazy Daisy

Continental

Cross-Stitch

1.

2.

Hem Stitch: This is often used to finish the edges of appliqué. Use thread to match the fabric. Bring the needle up from the wrong side of the fabric through the folded edge of the appliqué. Insert the needle on the diagonal into the top of the fabric close to the appliqué and slightly ahead of the first stitch.

Cross-stitch: This is another stitch used to finish the edges of an appliqué, but it is not invisible; it is used as a decoration. You can use matching thread or a contrasting color, and two strands of embroidery floss is a nice way to give the stitches character.

Stitch all lines slanted in the same direction around the edge of the appliqué. Then repeat in the opposite direction making a series of *X*'s all around.

Slip Stitch: When closing seams the slip stitch is usually recommended because it is invisible. Fold under the seam allowance on one side of the opening and pin it over the raw edge of the opposite side of the fabric.

Insert the needle through the bottom layer of fabric right at the seam line at one end of the opening. Take a small stitch through the fold on the top layer, then through the seam line on the bottom layer. Continue in this way so that the seam line matches the area that has been machine stitched from the wrong side.

Fabric

Cotton calico is the fabric used for all the projects included here. It is inexpensive and available in all fabric shops. While it comes 45 inches wide, I always use a 44-inch measure to allow for selvage. When I show a square wallhanging, for example, if it doesn't have borders the finished size will never be more than 42 inches square.

The colors of the calico fabric are varied and you will find a wide range of shades. In this way you can be creative without color limitations. The greatest appeal for calico is the small, overall prints that make a country statement. They all work together, which is most evident in an early American traditional quilt that utilizes several different prints and colors to create a patchwork design. Each fabric print seems to be balanced and in scale with the others.

I have found that it's a good idea to wash your fabric before making any project. Sometimes the fabric shrinks if it is 100 percent cotton, so this is best done before cutting out pattern pieces. The washing also removes any sizing and softens the fabric. The colors may fade slightly, which gives it a nicer look. Now and then I bleach the fabric when the colors are intense and I want to create the look of an antique.

Muslin is a good, inexpensive backing material and is often used for country projects. It comes 45, 52, and sometimes 60 inches wide, and sells for approximately three dollars a yard. It should be washed before using.

Making Pillow Piping

Contrasting or matching piping is a nice way to finish the edges of a pillow. Seat cushions are also crisp and professional-looking when trimmed with matching fabric-covered piping. The piping can be very narrow, as for a small throw pillow, or quite fat, if used as the trim on a floor-length tablecloth, for example. The cording for piping is sold by the yard in most fabric shops and is quite inexpensive. It looks like soft rope.

Measure around the pillow edge and add an extra inch. Cut lengths of bias fabric 1½ inches wide and stitch together to create a strip long enough to go around the pillow.

Turn one raw edge of fabric under ¼ inch and place cording in the center of the strip. Fold the fabric over the cording so the long, raw edges are aligned with cord encased inside.

Using a zipper foot on your sewing machine, stitch along the fabric as close to the cording as possible. When you get to the end, turn the raw fabric edge under, but do not stitch the last half inch of the fabric together. The cording will not reach the end of the fabric.

Begin at the center of one edge of the pillow top and pin piping all around with raw edges aligned. Where the two ends meet, overlap the extra fabric so that the cording comes together inside the fabric channel. Stitch around.

With right sides facing and raw edges aligned, pin the backing fabric piece to the top with the piping between. Stitch around 3 sides and 4 corners, leaving a few inches open on one side for turning. Trim the seam allowance and clip off the corners. Turn right-side out and finish the pillow as directed in each project.

For the Home

Breakfast Set

It's fun to dress up a table for Sunday brunch, breakfast for two, or just to lift your spirits. The cheerful yellow and blue calicos make an interesting combination, and the fat bows are the perfect feminine accents around the tablecloth. The pillow covers have bow tie closings to match. Make this complete set in an afternoon.

Tablecloth and Napkins: This tablecloth is 44 inches square, using the full width of a 45-inch fabric. The yellow trim is also used around the napkins and for the bow ties. It's an easy project and will fit a square or round table, alone or over another full-length cloth, as shown here.

Materials
2¼ yards blue calico
1 yard yellow calico

Directions
All measurements for cutting fabric include a ¼-inch seam allowance.

Cut the following:
blue calico
    1 square 44½ × 44½ inches
    4 squares 16½ × 16½ inches (4 napkins)
yellow calico
    4 pieces 1½ × 23½ inches
    2 pieces 1½ × 44½ inches
    8 pieces 1½ × 18½ inches
    8 pieces 1½ × 16½ inches
    4 pieces 4 × 34 inches

Directions

To make the tablecloth
1. With right sides facing and raw edges aligned, stitch the yellow border pieces (1½ × 44½ inches) to the top and bottom edges of the blue tablecloth square.
2. Next, join two strips 1½ × 23½ inches to make one longer strip. Repeat with the remaining two strips and join each strip to the sides of the blue square cloth. Open seams and press.
3. Fold the border edges under ¼ inch and

press. Fold under another ¼ inch, press and stitch around.

To make bows

1. With right sides facing, fold the yellow piece (4 × 34 inches) in half lengthwise.
2. Mark and cut both ends of the fabric at a slight angle.
3. Stitch across one short end and down the long edges.
4. Trim all seams and turn right-side out.
5. Turn the raw edges of the open short end to the inside and slip-stitch closed.
6. Tie the strip into a full bow. Make 4. Stitch a bow to the center of the border at each side of the tablecloth.

To make the napkins

1. With right sides facing and raw edges aligned, stitch the yellow border strips (1½ × 16½ inches) to the top and bottom edges of the 16½-inch square. Open seams and press.
2. Join side borders (1½ × 18½ inches) in the same way.
3. Fold the borders under ¼ inch and press. Fold under another ¼ inch all around and slip-stitch to the back of each napkin for a finished edge. Make 4.

Pillow Cover (14 × 14 inches)

Materials

1 yard yellow calico
14-inch pillow form

Directions

All fabric measurements include a ¼-inch seam allowance.

Cut the following:
2 squares 14½ × 14½ inches
12 strips 2¼ × 15 inches
2 pieces for lining 4 × 14½ inches

1. With right sides facing and raw edges aligned, pin 2 strips together.
2. Stitch down both long side edges and across one short end.
3. Turn right-side out and press. Make 6.
4. With right sides facing and raw edges aligned, pin 2 squares together and stitch around 3 sides.

5. Turn right-side out and press. Turn top raw edges under ¼ inch and press.
6. Turn top edges of lining to wrong side ¼ inch and press.
7. With right sides facing join front and back lining pieces at sides. Turn bottom raw edges under and stitch to make a finished hem.
8. Slip the lining inside top of pillow cover so that top edges match and side seams are aligned.
9. Slip the raw ends of the ties between the front and lining of the pillow on front and back so they are evenly spaced, with one set at each end and one set in the middle.
10. Insert pillow form and tie with bows to close.

Placemats (4)

Materials

¾ yard yellow calico
¾ yard blue fabric
thin quilt batting
tracing paper

Directions

1. Trace the pattern, which represents a quarter of the placemat, 4 times to make the full pattern, which includes a ¼-inch seam allowance.
2. Use the full pattern to cut 4 pieces from the yellow and 4 pieces from the blue fabric.
3. Cut 4 pattern pieces of thin batting.
4. With right sides facing and raw edges aligned, pin the fabric to a batting piece and stitch all around, leaving a small opening for turning.
5. Trim seams and turn right-side out. Press.
6. Turn raw edges to inside and slip-stitch closed. Make 4.

To finish

1. Machine-stitch ⅛ inch from outside edge all around.
2. Next, machine-stitch 1 inch from first seam all around. This finishes the placemat with a nice detail.

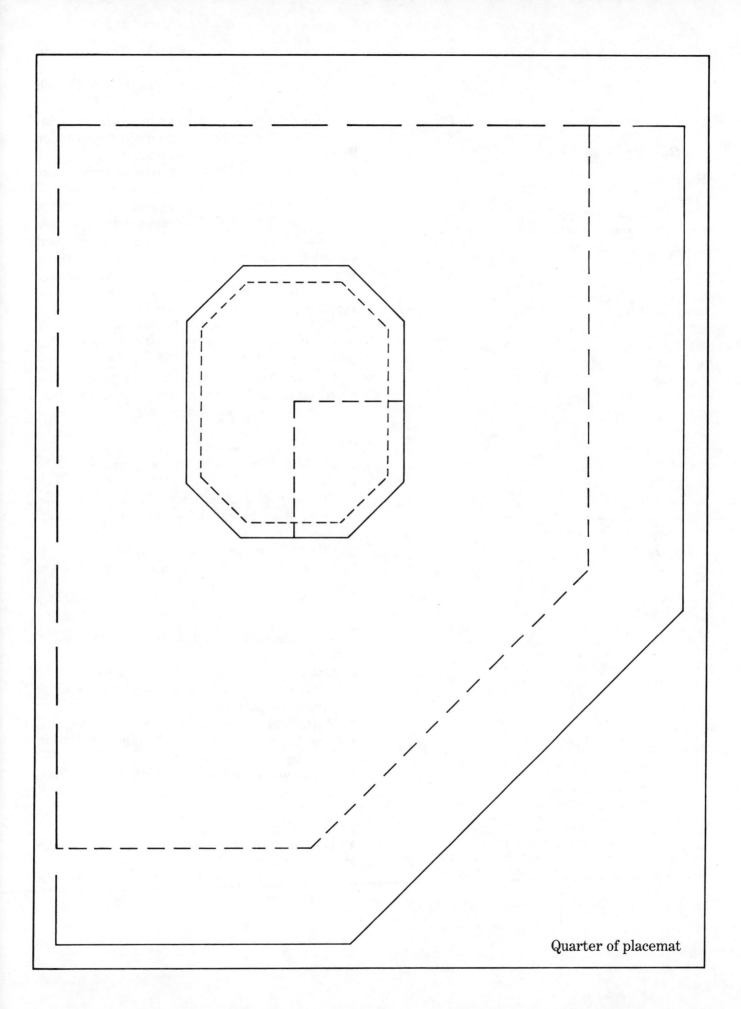

Quarter of placemat

Tea Cozy and Egg Cozy

Materials
¼ yard yellow calico
scrap of blue fabric
1 yard blue piping
thin quilt batting
tracing paper

Directions
Patterns include a ¼-inch seam allowance.

Tea Cozy
1. Place pattern on fold of yellow fabric and cut out. Make 2.
2. Cut 2 pieces of batting same size as pattern piece.
3. Pin fabric to batting and machine quilt with a 1-inch grid pattern on both pieces.
4. With edges matching, pin the piping around the front of the quilted fabric. Stitch around. (No piping across the bottom.)
5. Pin the backing fabric face down over the piped fabric and stitch around, leaving the bottom edge open. Turn to right side.

To finish
1. Fold the bottom edge under and slip-stitch to inside.
2. Cut a strip of blue fabric 1¼ × 2 inches for the tab. Fold in half lengthwise and turn raw edges to inside. Press.
3. Stitch along edge. Fold tab in half and stitch to the back of the top in the center of the tea cozy.

Egg Cozy
1. Trace the pattern and pin to the yellow fabric. Cut 2.
2. Cut 2 pieces of quilt batting same size.
3. Pin fabric to quilt batting and machine-quilt in a ½-inch grid pattern.
4. With right sides facing and raw edges aligned, pin the 2 pieces together with piping between. (No piping across bottom edge.)
5. Stitch all around, leaving bottom open. Turn right-side out.

To finish
1. Fold bottom edge under and slip-stitch to inside of egg cozy.
2. Cut a strip of blue fabric 1 × 1½ inches for tab. Finish as for tea cozy.

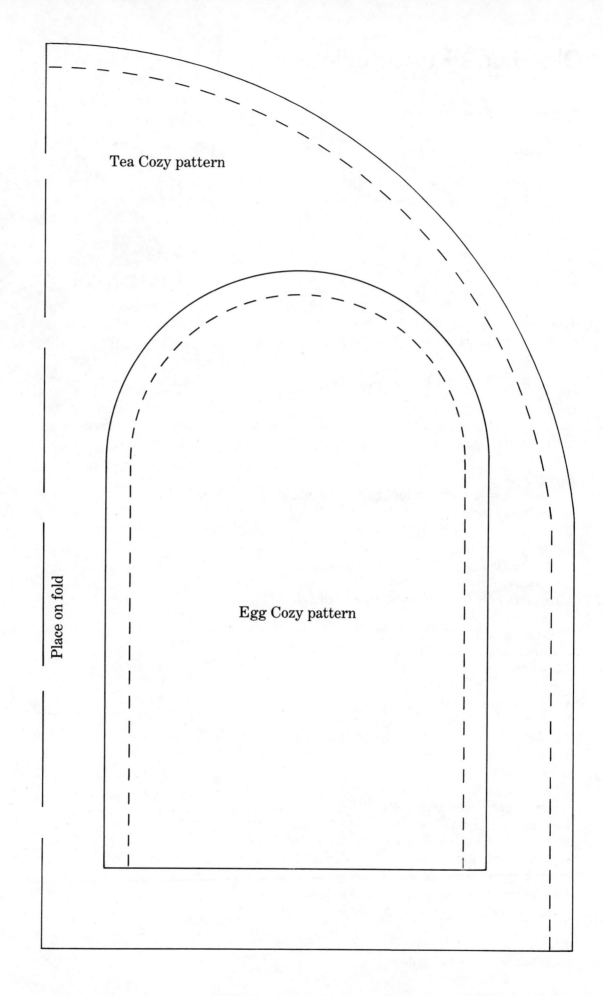

Tea Cozy pattern

Place on fold

Egg Cozy pattern

Old Maid's Puzzle Pillow

This easy patchwork quilt pattern is perfect for a throw pillow. Use scraps of fabric for an interesting and inexpensive project. The pillow is 16 by 16 inches, for which you can use a standard pillow form.

After you have made one square, you might like to repeat it in order to create a quilt. Each square can be divided with lattice strips (see Bear Paw Quilt on page 36).

Materials
scraps of light green calico (A) and solid light green fabric (B)
½ yard dark green fabric (C)
16-inch pillow form
thin quilt batting 16 × 16 inches
64 inches green piping
water soluble quilter's pen

Directions
All fabric measurements for cutting include a ¼-inch seam allowance.

Cut the following:
light green calico (A)
    4 squares 4½ × 4½ inches
    1 square 5 × 5 inches—cut into 2 triangles
      each
light green fabric (B)
    4 squares 5 × 5 inches—cut into 2 triangles
      each
dark green fabric (C)
    1 square 16½ × 16½ inches
    1 square 9 × 9 inches—cut into 2 triangles
    3 squares 5 × 5 inches—cut into 2 triangles
      each

1. With right sides facing and raw edges aligned, stitch a light green triangle (B) to the same size dark green triangle (C) along the diagonal to make a square. Make 4. Open seams and press.
2. With right sides facing and raw edges aligned, stitch a light green calico (A) to the same size dark green triangle (C) along the diagonal to make a square. Make 2. Open seams and press.

Old Maid's Puzzle Pillow

3. Join 2 light green triangles (B) to a calico/dark green square as shown in Figure 1. Make 2. Open seams and press.

4. Join large triangles together along the diagonal to make large squares (see Figure 1).

5. With right sides facing and raw edges aligned, join a green calico square (A) to a dark green/light green square. Next, join a dark green/light green square to a green calico square (A) (see Figure 2). Join all 4 together. Make 2.

6. With right sides facing and raw edges aligned, join the 4 large blocks as shown in Figure 3.

Quilting

1. Place top of pillow on batting piece and baste through both layers with long stitches from the center out, or pin all around.

2. Trace and transfer quilting patterns onto fabric with a washable pen or a light pencil (see Marking Patterns for Quilting, page 18 and Sources for Supplies, page 175, for pen).

3. Using small running stitches, quilt pillow from the center out on all marked lines. Or, for a quick quilting project, you can quilt ¼ inch on each side of all seam lines.

4. Remove basting stitches or pins and trim batting slightly smaller than pillow top.

To finish

1. With right sides facing and raw edges aligned, pin the piping around the pillow top. Stitch all around.

2. With right sides facing and raw edges aligned, pin the backing piece to the top of the pillow with the piping between. Stitch around 3 sides and 4 corners, using stitch lines from the piping as a guide.

3. Clip corners and trim seams. Turn right-side out and stuff.

4. Turn raw edges under and slip-stitch opening closed.

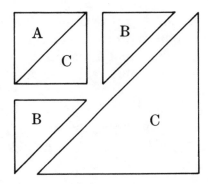

Figure 1   Make 2

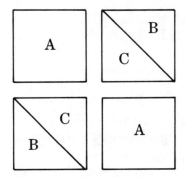

Figure 2   Make 2

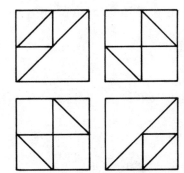

Figure 3   Joining blocks

Patchwork Pillow

This design is a variation on a traditional patchwork quilt pattern. It is a very easy project for a beginning quilter and is also a favorite among long-time quilters. It is created with small pieces of blue calico and solid fabrics but would be equally appealing in shades of red or green.

Our pillow is oversized at 20 by 20 inches and can be used on a couch or as a floor pillow.

Materials
(All fabric is 45 inches wide.)
¼ yard white fabric (A)
¼ yard light blue fabric (B)
½ yard light blue calico (C)
1 yard dark blue fabric (D)
thin quilt batting 21 × 21 inches
pillow form, 20 × 20 inches, or Poly-Fil™ stuffing

Directions
All fabric measurements for cutting include a ¼-inch seam allowance.

Cut the following:
white (A)
   1 square 5½ × 5½ inches
   4 squares 6 × 6 inches—cut into 2 triangles each
light blue (B)
   4 squares 5½ × 5½ inches
light blue calico (C)
   8 squares 6 × 6 inches—cut into 2 triangles each
dark blue (D)
borders:
   2 strips 4½ × 20½ inches
   2 strips 4½ × 28½ inches
   1 square 20½ × 20½ inches (backing)
   4 squares 5½ × 5½ inches
   4 squares 6 × 6 inches—cut into 2 triangles each

1. With right sides facing and raw edges aligned, stitch a light blue calico triangle (C) to a white triangle (A) along the diagonal to make a 5½-inch square. Make 8. Open seams and press.

Patchwork Pillow   Figure 2 Joining rows

34

2. With right sides facing and raw edges aligned, stitch a light blue calico triangle (C) to a dark blue triangle (D) along the diagonal to make a 5½-inch square. Make 8. Open seams and press.

3. Arrange squares as shown in Figure 1.

4. With right sides facing and raw edges aligned, join 5 squares, to make the first row across.

5. Continue to join squares to make 5 rows as shown in Figure 2.

6. With right sides facing and raw edges aligned, join all rows to form the pillow top. Open seams and press.

Quilting

1. Place top of pillow on batting piece and baste through both layers with long stitches from the center out, or pin all around.

2. Transfer quilting patterns onto fabric with the washable pen or a light pencil (see Marking Patterns for Quilting, page 18, and Sources for Supplies, page 175, for pen).

3. Using small running stitches, quilt pillow from center out, on all marked lines. Or, for a quick quilting project, you can quilt ¼ inch on each side of all seam lines.

4. Remove basting stitches or pins and trim batting slightly smaller than pillow top.

To finish

1. With wrong sides facing and raw edges aligned, stitch front of pillow to the backing piece around 3 sides.

2. With right sides facing and raw edges aligned, join short border strips to top and bottom edges of pillow top.

3. Join long border strips to each side edge.

4. Fold border in half all around so that you have a 2-inch border on the front and back of the pillow.

5. Turn raw edge under ¼ inch and press. Slip-stitch to back of pillow, leaving one side open.

6. Stuff pillow and slip-stitch open side closed.

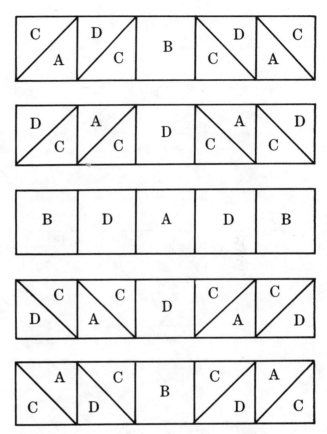

Figure 1

Bear Paw Quilt

This is a traditional early American quilt pattern. Its name will give you a clue to its origin. Paw prints found in the snow were an inspiration to our earliest quilt designers. It is most striking when done in one color with white. A faded rose, red, or blue are the most favored.

This quilt has been designed to fit a double- or queen-size bed and is 72 by 92 inches. You can add a wider border if you want to make the quilt larger.

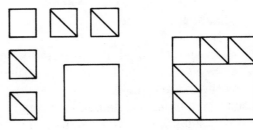

Figure 1

Materials
(All fabric is 45 inches wide.)
3 yards rose calico
5 yards solid white fabric
5¼ yards backing fabric (muslin is a good choice)
quilt batting
white thread
large hoop for quilting

Directions
All fabric measurements for cutting include ¼-inch seam allowance.

Cut the following:
rose calico borders:
    2 strips 1½ × 92½ inches
    2 strips 1½ × 74½ inches
    2 pieces 26 × 32 inches
    84 squares 4½ × 4½ inches
    50 squares 2½ × 2½ inches
solid white borders:
    2 strips 4½ × 82½ inches
    2 strips 4½ × 66½ inches
    49 pieces 2½ × 14½ inches
    80 pieces 2½ × 6½ inches
    80 squares 2½ × 2½ inches
    2 pieces 26 × 32 inches

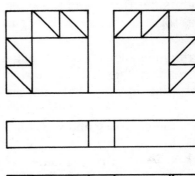

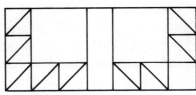

Quick and easy triangle method
Use this method for sewing triangles together (see page 19).

1. On wrong side of each 26 × 32-inch piece of white fabric, measure and mark off 3 × 3-inch

Block assembly   Figure 2

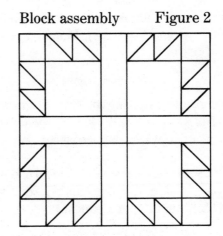

squares, so that you have 10 across and 8 down, for a total of 80 squares of each piece of fabric.

2. Draw diagonal lines through all squares in the same direction.

3. With right sides facing and raw edges aligned, pin the marked-off white fabric to the piece of rose calico the same size.

4. Stitch ¼ inch on each side of all diagonal lines.

5. Cut on all solid lines. Open seams and press. You will have 320 squares made from rose calico and white squares.

To make a block

1. With right sides facing and raw edges aligned, stitch pieces together as shown in Figure 1. Make 4.

2. With right sides facing and raw edges aligned, join 2 squares together with a short (2½ × 6½ inches) white lattice strip between as shown in Figure 2.

3. With right sides facing and raw edges aligned, join 2 white lattice strips (2½ × 6½ inches) together with a 2½-inch rose square between, as shown in Figure 2.

4. Repeat step 2, as shown in Figure 2.

5. Join all squares to form a block (see Figure 2). Open all seams and press. Makes 20 blocks.

To make rows

1. With right sides facing and raw edges aligned, join a white lattice strip (2½ × 14½ inches) to the left edge of block.

2. Continue to join blocks separated by lattice strips in this way. There are 4 blocks and 5 lattice strips per row (see Figure 3). Make 5 rows. Open seams and press.

To make a sash

1. With right sides facing and raw edges aligned, stitch a rose square (2½ × 2½ inches) to one short edge of a white lattice strip (2½ × 14½ inches).

2. Continue to join lattice strips to rose squares in this way, using 4 strips and 5 squares (see Figure 4). Make 6. Open seams and press.

Joining rows
1. With right sides facing and raw edges aligned, join one divider strip to the top edge of Row 1.
2. With right sides facing and raw edges aligned, continue to join rows in this way. Open seams and press.

Joining rows   Figure 3

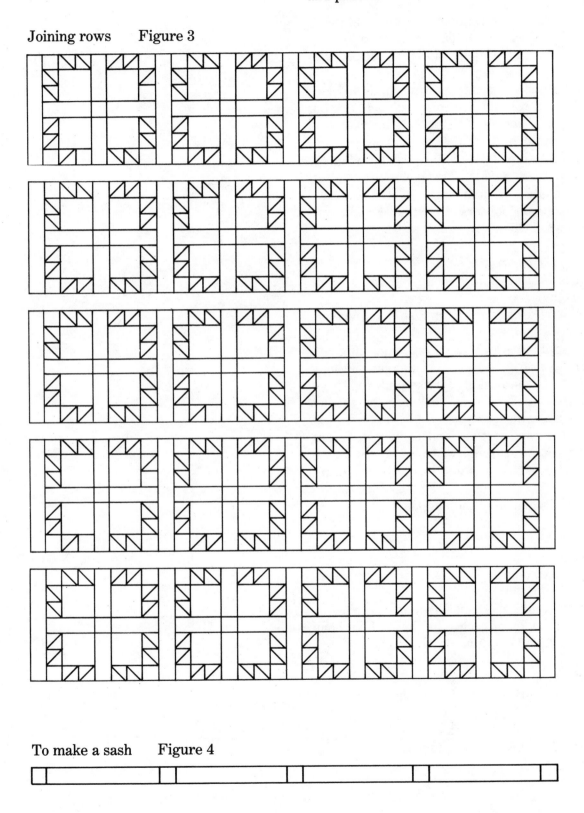

To make a sash   Figure 4

Borders

1. With right sides facing and raw edges aligned, join white border (4½ × 66½ inches) to the top and bottom edges of quilt top. Open seams and press.

2. With right sides facing and raw edges aligned, join a 4½-inch rose square to the top and bottom edges of white borders (4½ × 82½ inches). Join to sides of quilt top. Open seams and press.

3. With right sides facing and raw edges aligned, join rose borders (1½ × 74¼ inches) to the top and bottom edges of quilt top.

4. Join rose side borders (1½ × 92½ inches) in the same way. Open seams and press.

Preparing the backing

1. Cut the batting ¼ inch smaller than the quilt top all around.

2. Cut the backing fabric in half, so that you have 2 pieces 2⅝ yards each.

3. With right sides facing and raw edges aligned, stitch these two pieces together along one long edge to create the backing for the quilt top.

4. Trim down both sides of backing piece so that it is 77 inches wide.

5. Baste the top, batting, and backing together with long stitches through all three layers. Begin at the center of the quilt and baste to each outer corner.

6. Pin or baste around the outside edges, it necessary.

Quilting

1. Use an extra-large hoop and secure on a center block.

2. To hand quilt, use small running stitches ¼ inch on both sides of each seam line. Move hoop to next block and continue.

To finish

1. When all quilting is complete, remove all basting stitches.

2. Fold the raw edges of the top and backing in ¼ inch and press. Stitch together with a slip stitch.

Appliqué Tablecloth and Napkins

This pretty rose appliqué with leaves and buds is reminiscent of a stencil design. It's easy to apply fabric to fabric with iron-on fusible webbing. The tablecloth can be made to fit your table's dimensions using two matching fabrics in the color of your choice. The roses are cut from a similar pink calico print to match the green fabric. A small bud and leaf are applied to each napkin.

Materials (45-inch-wide fabric)
To determine how much fabric to buy for the tablecloth top, measure the width and length of your table and deduct 4 inches in each direction for a 2-inch border all around.

Border: This tablecloth has an 8-inch border with 2 inches on the top of the table and a 6-inch drop. If you want more of a drop, determine this and add extra inches.

Appliqué:
¼ yard fabric
fusible webbing
tracing paper

Directions
1. Cut lighter fabric for the top of the table.
2. Cut 2 border strips from darker fabric 8½ inches × the width of your table plus ½ inch for seams.
3. Cut 2 more border pieces from dark fabric 8½ inches × the length of your table plus 16½ inches.
4. With right sides facing and raw edges aligned, join the top and bottom border pieces to each short end of the top fabric piece. Open seams and press.
5. Join side border pieces in the same way.
6. Turn all raw edges under ¼ inch all around and press. Fold edges under another ¼ inch and stitch all around for a finished edge.

To make appliqués
1. Enlarge the design on tracing paper (see page

13) and make 2 tracings. One is for cutting, the other for placement.

2. Cut away the roses and pin to pink fabric on top of fusible webbing. Cut out 2 of each.

3. Pin stems and leaves to dark fabric on top of fusible webbing. Cut out 2 of each.

4. Position the full pattern tracing as shown in Figure 1.

5. Pin each appliqué piece in position under the tracing. Remove the tracing and fuse fabrics together using a medium-hot iron.

Napkins

Each napkin is 17 × 17 inches. Directions are given to make 4.

Cut the following:

All fabric measurements include ¼-inch seam allowance.

dark green calico
  4 squares 16½ × 16½ inches

light green calico
  8 strips 1¼ × 16½ inches
  8 strips 1¼ × 18 inches

1. With right sides facing and raw edges aligned, join a light green strip 1¼ × 16½ inches to one edge of a dark green square. Join another light green strip to the opposite side of the square.

2. Next join a light green strip 1¼ × 18 inches to the remaining sides of the dark green square. Open seams and press.

3. Fold the raw edges under ¼ inch and press. Fold edges under another ¼ inch and stitch all around entire square.

To appliqué

1. Trace one leaf, stem, and bud.

2. Pin stem and leaf to green calico and fusible webbing and cut out. Make 4.

3. Repeat for buds in a pink fabric.

4. Position each appliqué in the corner of each napkin and fuse with medium-hot iron.

Note: Fusible webbing and appliqués will not come off when tablecloth is washed. Repeated washings in hot water, however, will loosen some edges if not secured properly. It is easy to repair by slipping a small piece of the webbing under the appliqué and fusing with a hot iron where needed.

Each square equals 1 inch

Cut 2 of each

Tablecloth Appliqué pattern

Welcome Wallhanging   Figure 1

Welcome Wallhanging

Make a colorful country wallhanging using zig-zag appliqué. This is a good housewarming gift or use it in your home to welcome guests. The finished size is 18 by 31 inches which is a good size for a mantel or door.

Materials
small amount of white fabric
¼ yard red calico
¼ yard green calico
½ yard light blue fabric
1 yard dark blue calico (includes backing)
½ yard thin quilt batting
wooden dowel, 1 inch in diameter, 33 inches
    long
tracing paper
stiff paper
nylon thread for hanging

Directions
All patterns are shown full size.
1. Trace and transfer pattern pieces C and D to stiff paper to make templates (see page 14).
2. Trace each letter of WELCOME and use these patterns to cut each letter from the dark blue calico.

Cut the following:
All fabric measurements for cutting include a ¼-inch seam allowance where necessary.
light blue
    3 squares 9½ × 9½ inches
    1 piece 6½ × 29½ inches
green calico
    13 strips 1½ × 9½ inches
    2 strips 1½ × 6½ inches
    4 strips 2½ × 4½ inches (hanging tabs)
red calico
    12 squares 1½ × 1½ inches
    3 squares ¾ × ¾ inches (A)
    3 pieces 3¾ × 4 inches (B)
    3 pieces (C)
    3 pieces (D)
dark blue calico
    1 piece 18½ × 31½ inches (backing)
white

3 pieces 1⅛ × 2¾ inches (E)
6 pieces 1 × 1⅞ inches (F)
batting
18 × 31 inches

To appliqué
1. Refer to Figure 1 for diagram of completed project.
2. Pin 2 F pieces in position on each B piece as shown in Figure 2.
3. Pin an E piece on each C piece as shown in Figure 2.
4. Using matching thread and a narrow zigzag stitch, sew around each E and F piece.
5. Pin pieces A, B, C, and D in place on each light blue 9½-inch square as shown in Figure 2.
6. Using matching thread and a narrow zigzag stitch, sew around all A, B, C, and D pieces.
7. Beginning and ending 2 inches from each side edge, pin each letter so they are evenly spaced on the 6½- × -29½-inch light blue strip.
8. Using navy blue thread and a narrow zigzag stitch, sew around each letter.

Joining house squares
1. With right sides facing and raw edges aligned, join a green lattice strip 1½ × 9½ inches to one side edge of house square. Open seams and press.
2. Continue joining house squares with green strips between. Open seams and press.

Making borders
1. With right sides facing and raw edges aligned, join a 1½-inch red square to one short end of a green strip (1½ × 9½ inches).
2. Continue in this way with 2 more strips separated by 3 more red squares. Make 3. Open seams and press.

To assemble
1. With right sides facing and raw edges aligned, join border strip to the top edge of the house strip. Open seams and press.
2. Join border strip to the bottom edge of house strip in the same way.

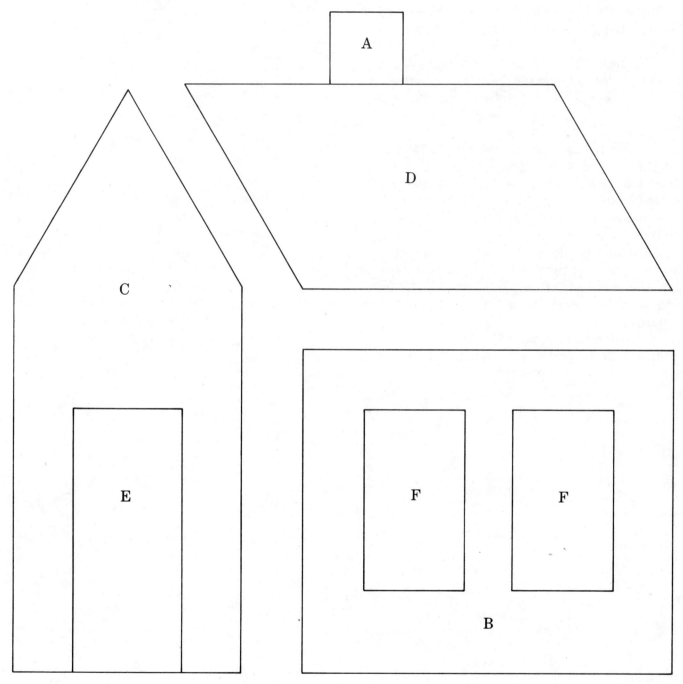

Figure 2

47

3. Next, join the WELCOME strip, followed by a border strip, as shown in finished diagram Figure 1.

4. With right sides facing and raw edges aligned, fold fabric for hanging tabs in half lengthwise and stitch along edge. Turn right-side out and press.

To finish

1. With *wrong* sides facing and batting between, pin the top and backing fabric together.

2. Stitch around each appliqué square in the seam line to quilt.

3. Remove pins and trim batting ¼ inch all around.

4. Turn all raw edges under ¼ inch and press.

5. Fold hanging tabs in half lengthwise and insert the raw ends of each tab between the front and back of fabric at each top edge of a red square. Pin in position.

6. Slip-stitch all around.

7. Insert dowel and hang with nylon thread.

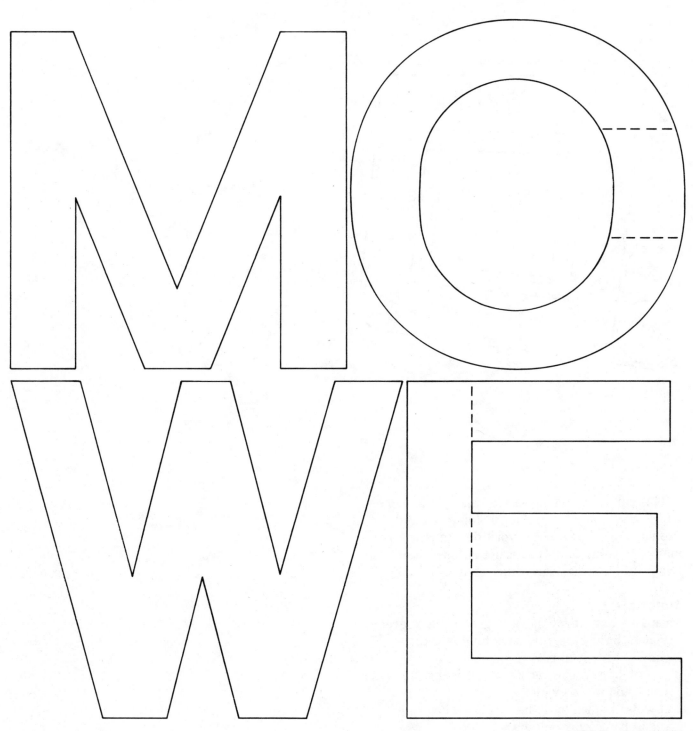

Make *L* from *E*

Log Cabin Log Carrier

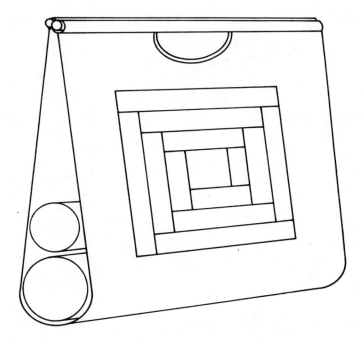

This canvas-lined log carrier is 22 by 44 inches, which is an ample size for holding a bundle of fireplace logs. The patchwork design is the popular log cabin quilt pattern that is made from scraps of light and dark calico strips.

Materials

scraps of dark brown, light green, dark green, peach, light blue, and dark blue fabrics
1 yard solid tan fabric
piece of heavy canvas 22 × 46 inches (canvas comes 54 inches wide)
2 dowels, ¾-inch in diameter, 22 inches long
1 yard brown bias binding
stiff paper

Directions

All measurements for cutting fabric include a ¼-inch seam allowance.

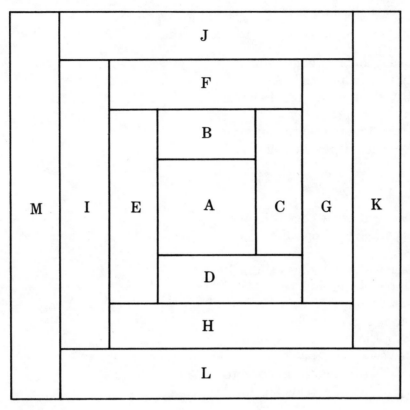

Figure 1

Cut the following:
dark brown
   3½- × -3½-inch square (center) (A)
   1 piece 2 × 8 inches (H)
   1 piece 2 × 9½ inches (I)
light green
   1 piece 2 × 3½ inches (B)
   1 piece 2 × 5 inches (C)
dark green
   1 piece 2 × 5 inches (D)
   1 piece 2 × 6½ inches (E)
peach
   1 piece 2 × 6½ inches (F)
   1 piece 2 × 8 inches (G)
light blue
   1 piece 2 × 9½ inches (J)
   1 piece 2 × 11 inches (K)
navy blue
   1 piece 2 × 11 inches (L)

1 piece 2 × 12½ inches (M)
solid tan for background
  2 pieces 6 × 12½ inches (sides)
  1 piece 7 × 23½ inches (top)
  1 piece 10½ × 23½ inches (bottom)
  1 piece 19 × 23½ inches (back)

Log cabin block

1. With right sides facing and raw edges aligned, join B to A along long edge. Open and press.
2. Next, join C to BA along long edge a shown in Figure 1. Open seams and press.
3. Continue to sew strips together until you have a square 12½ × 12½ inches. Open all seams and press.

Borders

1. With right sides facing and raw edges aligned, join tan side pieces to each side of log cabin block. Open seams and press.
2. With right sides facing and raw edges aligned, join top tan piece to top of log cabin block.
3. Repeat with bottom strip.
4. With right sides facing and raw edges aligned, join the back piece with the bottom edge of bottom border strip. Open seams and press.
5. With wrong sides facing, pin outside fabric to canvas lining, with 1½ inches of outside fabric all around.
6. Fold top and bottom edges of top over canvas lining with a ¾-inch seam allowance and stitch.
7. Turn raw edges of top sides under ¼ inch and press. Turn over ½ inch and stitch along sides.
8. Fold top and bottom edges another 1 inch and sew along edge to create a ¾-inch channel for the dowels.

To finish

1. Cut a 4-inch circle from stiff paper. Cut circle in half.
2. Center each half circle on the top and bottom of the log carrier as shown in Figure 2 and trace around it on the fabric.
3. Cut out each half circle and finish the edges with bias binding.
4. Place dowels through the channels and fold carrier in half.

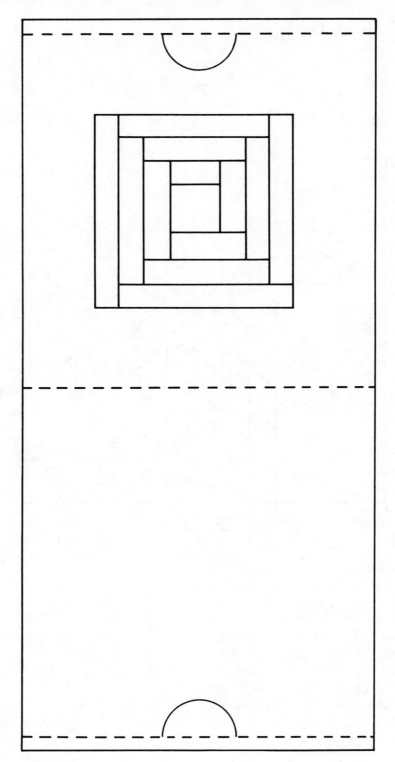

Figure 2

Lone Star Tablecloth

Lone Star Tablecloth

The star pattern is a traditional quilt design and is found on pillows, wallhangings, and tablecloths as well. This one was designed as an overskirt for a small, round candle table. It is 31 by 31 inches and will fit the top of a bridge table as well.

Materials
¼ yard maroon fabric (A)
¼ yard white calico (B)
¼ yard blue fabric (C)
¼ yard tan calico (D)
¼ yard rose fabric (E)
⅔ yard navy blue fabric (F)
tracing paper
stiff paper for template

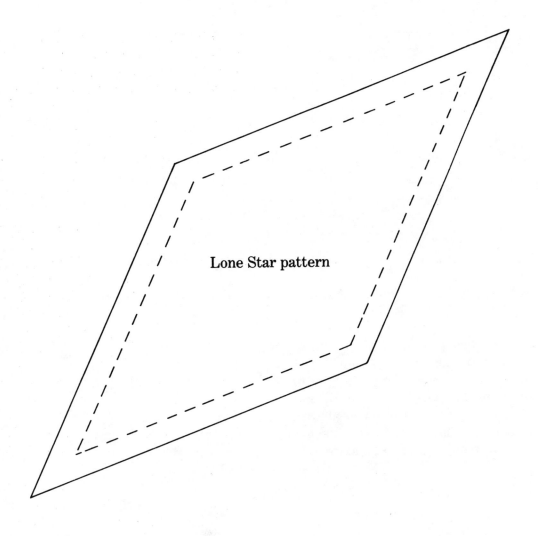

Lone Star pattern

Directions

All measurements for cutting fabric include a ¼-inch seam allowance.

1. Trace and transfer the pattern to stiff paper for a template (see page 14).

Use the template to cut the following:

(A)   8 pattern pieces
(B)   16 pattern pieces
(C)   24 pattern pieces
(D)   16 pattern pieces
(E)   8 pattern pieces
(F)   4 squares 9½ × 9½ inches
        2 squares 10 × 10 inches—cut into 2 triangles each

2. With right sides facing and raw edges aligned,

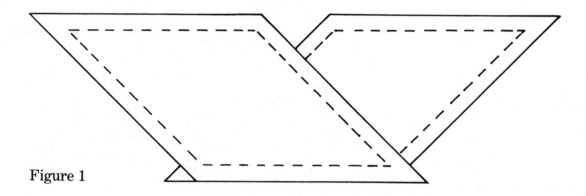

Figure 1

join C to D along short edge as shown in Figure 1.

3. Next join CD to E for a row of 3 pieces.

4. With right sides facing and raw edges aligned, join B to C to D in the same way for Row 2.

5. Next, join A to B to C in the same way for Row 3. Open seams and press.

6. With right sides facing and raw edges aligned, join Row 1 to Row 2, followed by Row 3 as shown in Figure 2. Open seams and press. Make 8.

Figure 2   Make 8

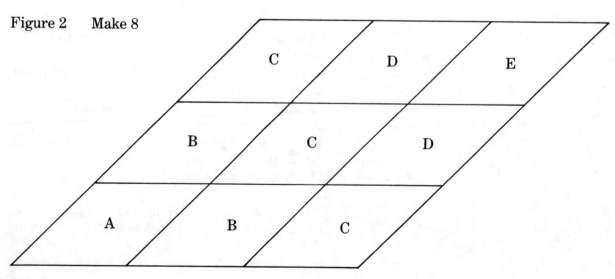

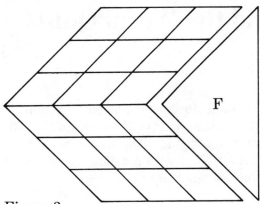

Figure 3

Assembling star
1. With right sides facing and raw edges aligned, join 2 star pieces with a navy (F) triangle according to Figure 3.
2. Repeat with remaining star pieces and triangles.
3. Join all star pieces with navy (F) squares as shown in Figure 4.

To finish
1. Fold raw edges under ¼ inch all around and press.
2. Fold under another ¼ inch and stitch all around.

Figure 4

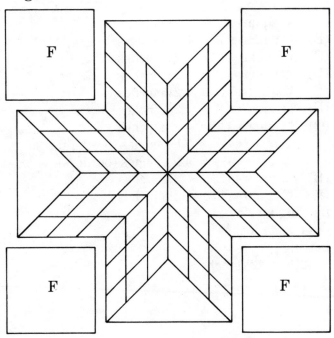

Around the World Quilt

Susan Fernald Joyce used a combination of light and dark blues and pinks to create this 43-inch-square wallhanging. The 4-inch-wide borders are hand quilted with a delicate continuous vine and heart-shaped leaves.

Materials
¼ yard each of the following fabrics:
    navy blue calico (A)
    blue-violet calico (B)
    blue calico (C)
    light blue fabric (D)
    navy blue fabric (E)
    dark pink fabric (F)
⅔ yard peach fabric (G)
¼ yard blue checked fabric (H)
¼ yard violet fabric (I)
1¼ yards backing fabric
thin quilt batting
tracing paper
water soluble quilter's pen

Directions
All fabric measurements for cutting include a ¼-inch seam allowance.

Cut the following:
(A) 33 squares 2½ × 2½ inches
(B) 32 squares 2½ × 2½ inches
(C) 32 squares 2½ × 2½ inches
(D) 32 squares 2½ × 2½ inches
(E) 32 squares 2½ × 2½ inches
(F) 32 squares 2½ × 2½ inches
(G) 32 squares 2½ × 2½ inches
      2 pieces 4½ × 34½ inches (borders)
      2 pieces 4½ × 42½ inches (borders)
(H) 32 squares 2½ × 2½ inches
(I)   32 squares 2½ × 2½ inches
backing fabric
   44 × 44 inches
batting
   42½ × 42½ inches

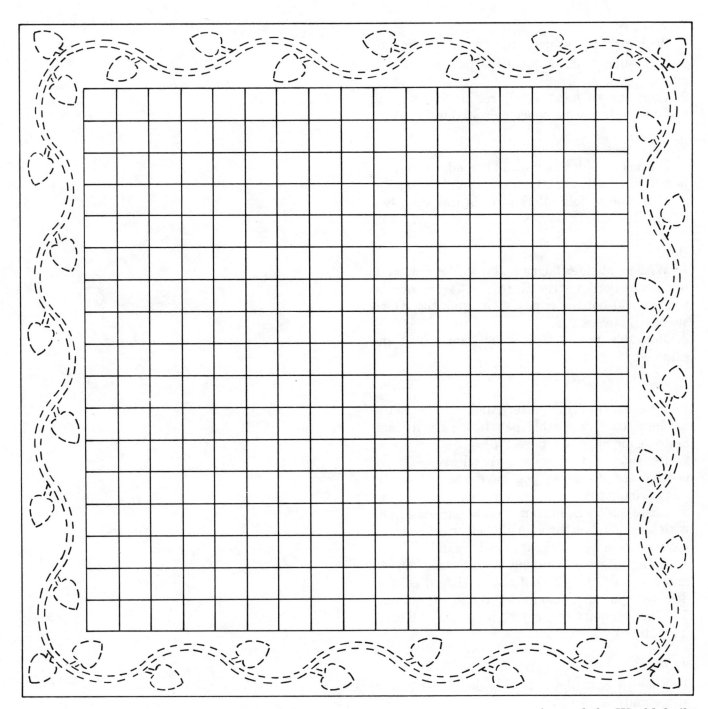

Around the World Quilt

59

To make rows

1. With right sides facing and raw edges aligned, join H square to G square. Open seams and press.
2. Continue to join 17 squares in this way to make rows in the sequence indicated in Figure 1.

To join rows

1. With right sides facing and raw edges aligned, join Row 1 to Row 2. Open seams and press.
2. Continue to join all 17 rows in this way. See Figure 1.

Borders

1. With right sides facing and raw edges aligned, join peach border strip (G) (4½ × 34½ inches) to the top and bottom edges of the quilt top. Open seams and press.
2. Join side pieces (4½ × 42½ inches) in the same way.

Quilting

1. Trace the quilting pattern and transfer to the borders using washable pen (see page 14 and Sources for Supplies, page 175).
2. Repeat the border pattern all around, connecting the stems so you have one continuous stem around the entire border area.
3. Baste quilt top, batting, and backing together with long stitches through all 3 layers. The backing piece will be 1 inch larger all around.
4. Using a small running stitch, quilt on all marked lines. Use a contrasting thread color if desired. Quilt diagonal lines through all squares.
5. When all quilting is complete, remove all basting stitches.

To finish

1. Fold the raw edges of the backing over ¼ inch all around and press.
2. Next, fold the edges of the backing piece over ½ inch to the front of the quilt top to create a ¼-inch border all around. Press and pin.
3. Slip-stitch all around.

H	G	F	E	D	C	B	A	I	A	B	C	D	E	F	G	H
G	F	E	D	C	B	A	I	H	I	A	B	C	D	E	F	G
F	E	D	C	B	A	I	H	G	H	I	A	B	C	D	E	F
E	D	C	B	A	I	H	G	F	G	H	I	A	B	C	D	E
D	C	B	A	I	H	G	F	E	F	G	H	I	A	B	C	D
C	B	A	I	H	G	F	E	D	E	F	G	H	I	A	B	C
B	A	I	H	G	F	E	D	C	D	E	F	G	H	I	A	B
A	I	H	G	F	E	D	C	B	C	D	E	F	G	H	I	A
I	H	G	F	E	D	C	B	A	B	C	D	E	F	G	H	I
A	I	H	G	F	E	D	C	B	C	D	E	F	G	H	I	A
B	A	I	H	G	F	E	D	C	D	E	F	G	H	I	A	B
C	B	A	I	H	G	F	E	D	E	F	G	H	I	A	B	C
D	C	B	A	I	H	G	F	E	F	G	H	I	A	B	C	D
E	D	C	B	A	I	H	G	F	G	H	I	A	B	C	D	E
F	E	D	C	B	A	I	H	G	H	I	A	B	C	D	E	F
G	F	E	D	C	B	A	I	H	I	A	B	C	D	E	F	G
H	G	F	E	D	C	B	A	I	A	B	C	D	E	F	G	H

To join rows   Figure 1

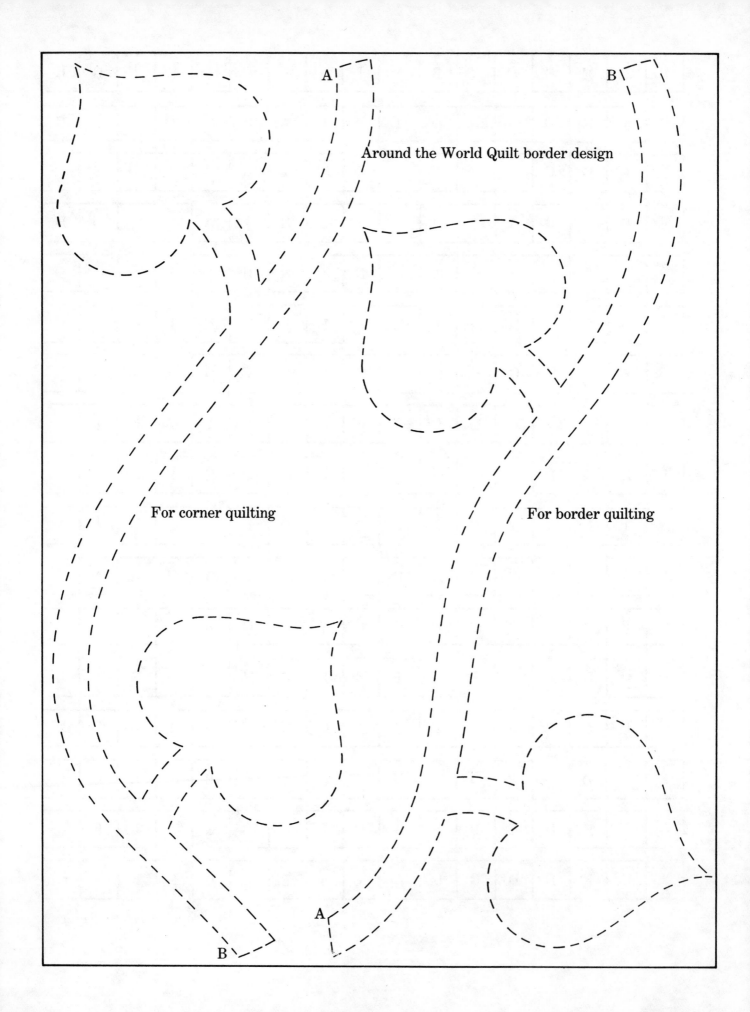

A B

Around the World Quilt border design

For corner quilting   For border quilting

A

B A

For Baby

ABC Quilt

This ABC bear fabric is called V. I. B., which stands for Very Important Bears and is the creation of V.I.P. Fabrics (A Division of Cranston Print Works). The red, white, or blue backgrounds are covered with an overall bear print. The alphabet squares feature a letter with a bear in a different position in the center of each. You can use the squares for framing, for quilt squares, or to make pillows.
The quilt is 33 × 42 inches.

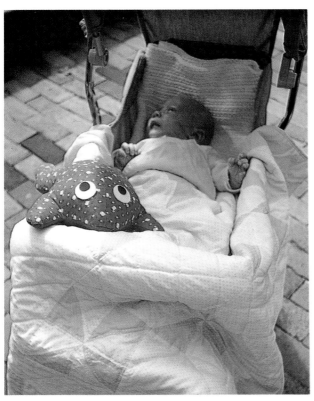

Bear Paw Quilt (page 36)   Patchwork Pillow (page 34)   Old Maid's Puzzle Pillow (page 32)

Appliqué Tablecloth and Napkins (page 41)

Breakfast Set (page 26)

Around the World Quilt (page 58)

Quilted Desk Set (page 114)

Welcome Wallhanging (page 45)   Log Cabin Log Carrier (page 50)   Lone Star Tablecloth (page 54)

Patchwork Teddy Bear (page 94)   Patchwork Baby Jacket (page 91)

Whimsical Pillow Toys (page 76)

Schoolhouse Pillow (page 118)

Clutch Purse (page 100)   Tissue Box Cover (page 104)   Eyeglass Case (page 107)

Heart Wallhanging (page 110)   Shoo-Fly Pillows (page 108)

Scented Fabric Hangers (page 150)   Cosmetic Bags (page 152)

Patchwork Potholders (page 154)

Lined Baskets (page 153)

Braided Wreath (page 135)

Cookie Cutter Ornaments (page 137)

Patchwork Tote (page 123)

Heart Wreath (page 132) Noel Banner (page 128)

Elf Stocking (page 142)
Patchwork Heart Pillow (page 140)

Pastel Lacy Stocking (page 145)
Patchwork Heart Pillow (page 140)

Appliqué Carryall (page 162)
Whimsical Bibs (page 158)

Beanbags (page 165)

Materials

1 panel V. I. B. red alphabet fabric

¼ yard red fabric with white hearts (alphabet borders)

⅔ yard white fabric with bear print (quilt square 1)

⅓ yard blue fabric with bear print (quilt square 2)

1¼ yards red fabric with bear print (borders)

thin quilt batting for crib size

1 yard backing fabric

Directions

All measurements for cutting include ¼-inch seam allowance.

Cut the following:
red heart fabric
    6 strips 1¾ × 6½ inches
    6 strips 1¾ × 9½ inches
white bear fabric
    6 squares 9½ inches
blue bear fabric
    4 squares 9½ inches
alphabet panels
    A square 7 × 7 inches
    B square 7 × 7 inches
    C square 7 × 7 inches
red bear print
    2 pieces 3½ × 27½ inches (cut across fabric)
    2 pieces 3½ × 42½ inches (cut down fabric)

To make alphabet blocks

1. With right sides facing and raw edges aligned, join a short red border strip to the top and bottom edge of the A square.

2. Next, join a long red border strip to the sides in the same way. Open all seams and press.

3. Repeat steps 1 and 2 with the B and C squares (see Figure 1).

Figure 1

To make rows

Row 1: With right sides facing and raw edges aligned, join square 1 to square 2, followed by another square 1. Open seams and press.

Row 2: With right sides facing and raw edges aligned, join the A square to a square 1, followed by the C square. Open seams and press.

Row 3: With right sides facing and raw edges aligned, join a square 1 to the B square, followed by another square 1. Open seams and press.

Row 4: With right sides facing and raw edges aligned, join a square 2 to a square 1, followed by a square 2. Open seams and press (see Figure 2).

To join rows

1. With right sides facing and raw edges aligned, join Row 1 to Row 2 along top long edge. Open seams and press.

2. Continue to join rows in this way until all 4 rows are joined. Open seams and press.

Border

1. With right sides facing and raw edges aligned, join the short red border strips to the top and bottom edges of the quilt top. Open seams and press.

2. Join side pieces in the same way (see Figure 3).

Quilting

1. Cut the batting ¼ inch smaller than the quilt top all around.

2. Cut backing fabric 33½ × 42½ inches.

3. Baste the top, batting, and backing together with long stitches through all three layers.

4. Machine-stitch along seam lines of each square and borders. Do not stitch into seam allowance all around outside edge. To quilt by hand, take short, even stitches ¼ inch on each side of all seams (see page 17).

To finish

1. Remove all basting stitches.

2. Fold raw edges of the top of the quilt under ¼ inch and press. Fold raw edges of backing to inside and press.

3. Stitch all around with slip stitch to close.

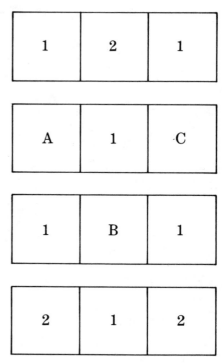

Figure 2   To make rows

Figure 3   Joining borders

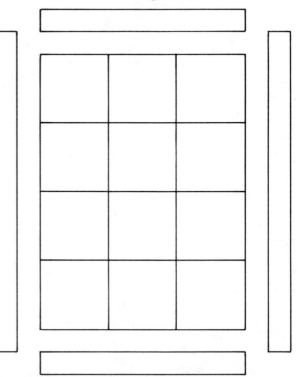

Alphabet Pillow

Alphabet pillow

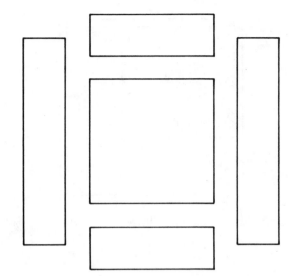

Figure 1

Using V. I. B. fabric make a 12-inch alphabet pillow for a crib or carriage. Each letter comes with a bear in a different position. You can choose the baby's initial for a personalized gift. This fabric comes in different colors, so you have a choice, and the borders of white hearts are printed on navy, light blue, red, and pink, to match the letter squares.

Materials
1 alphabet square
½ yard red fabric for heart
small amount of blue fabric for piping
50 inches thin cording
12-inch pillow form or Poly-Fil™ stuffing

Directions
All cutting includes ¼-inch seam allowance.

Cut the following:
letter square
   7 inches
red heart borders
   1 square 12½ inches (for back)

2 strips 3¼ × 6½ inches
2 strips 3¼ × 12½ inches

1. With right sides facing and raw edges aligned, join short red strips to the top and bottom edges of the letter square. Open seams and press.
2. Join long strips to the sides of the letter square in the same way. Open seams and press (see Figure 1).
3. Cut and piece blue fabric to create a strip 1½ × 50 inches for the piping.
4. To make piping see page 23, or you can buy premade piping in color of your choice.
5. With right sides facing and raw edges aligned, pin the piping around the front of the pillow. Stitch around. Remove pins.
6. With right sides facing and raw edges aligned, pin the pillow top to the backing, with the piping between.
7. Using the stitch line of the piping as a guide, stitch around, leaving one side open for stuffing.
8. Trim seams, clip corners, and turn right-side out. Stuff with pillow form or Poly-Fil™ stuffing and turn raw edges under. Slip-stitch closed.

Bear Patch Pillow

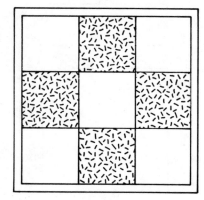

Bear Patch Pillow

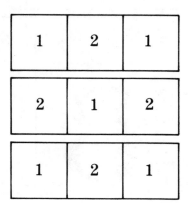

Figure 1

This little 9-patch pillow is easy to make, and you have a choice of red and white or blue and white color scheme. The little bears holding hearts and alphabet blocks are part of the panel of alphabets in the V. I. B. fabric series from V. I. P. used for the quilt on page 64. When we made the quilt we cut away the border of bears and just used the alphabet squares. The little bear squares on this 10½ × 10½-inch pillow are made from the leftovers. This is the perfect crib or carriage pillow to go with the alphabet quilt.

Materials
strip of bear fabric from the alphabet panel (A)
⅓ yard blue fabric for heart (B)
44 inches red piping
Poly-Fil™ stuffing

Directions
All measurements for cutting include a ¼-inch seam allowance.

Cut the following:
bear strip (A)
   5 squares 4 × 4 inches (each square will have
     2 bears)
blue heart fabric
   1 square 11 × 11 inches (for back)
   4 squares 4 × 4 inches

To make rows
Row 1: With right sides facing and raw edges aligned, join a bear square (A) to a blue square (B) followed by a bear square (A). Open seams and press.
Row 2: With right sides facing and raw edges aligned, join a blue square (B) to a bear square (A) followed by a blue square (B). Open seams and press.
Row 3: Repeat Row 1 (see Figure 1).

To join rows
1. With right sides facing and raw edges aligned, join Row 1 to Row 2. Open seams and press.
2. Join Row 2 to Row 3 in the same way.

To finish
1. With right sides facing and raw edges aligned, pin the piping to the pillow top all around. Stitch around and remove pins.
2. With right sides facing and raw edges aligned, pin the pillow to the backing with piping between. Stitch around, leaving one side open for turning.
3. Trim seams and clip corners. Turn and stuff.
4. Turn raw edges under ¼ inch and slip-stitch opening closed.

Hanging Hearts

A chain of stuffed hearts decorates the side of the crib and can also be used as a mobile to hang from one side of the crib to the other. The fabric matches the quilt and pillows, and you can make as many as needed to stretch from one side of the crib to the other.

Materials (for 3 hearts)
small amount of red fabric
1½ yards ½-inch satin ribbon
Poly-Fil™ stuffing
tracing paper
stiff paper for templates
ballpoint pen

Hanging Hearts heart pattern

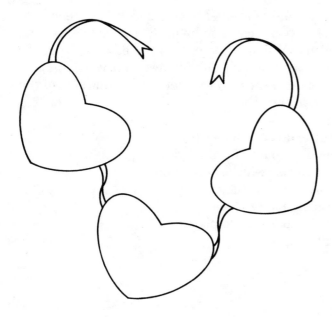

Directions

All patterns include ¼-inch seam allowance.

1. Trace the heart pattern and transfer to stiff paper for template (see page 14).
2. Place the template on the wrong side of red fabric and trace around outline. Make 6.
3. Cut out fabric hearts.
4. With right sides facing and raw edges aligned, pin a front and back heart together. Stitch around, leaving a small opening for turning and stuffing.
5. Repeat steps 3 and 4 for 2 more hearts.

To finish

1. Trim seams and clip around curves. Turn right-side out and stuff until full.
2. Turn raw edges under ¼ inch to inside and slip-stitch opening closed.
3. Place the satin ribbon on a table and position the hearts in the center so they are evenly spaced with approximately 2 inches between each one.
4. Pin the ribbon to the back of each heart and hold up the row of hearts. Check to be sure they are balanced and adjust accordingly. Tack ribbon to the back of each heart.

Crib Bumpers

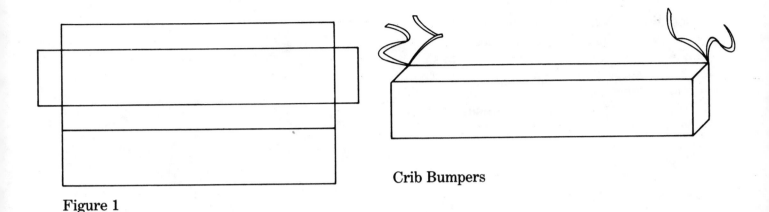

Figure 1

Crib Bumpers

The print used to cover these crib bumpers matches the quilt and crib pillows on page 66. You can find 2-inch thick foam in most five-and-tens or fabric shops, and it is easy to cut the exact length and width needed for your crib. When you consider how expensive crib bumpers are to buy, it's worth the small amount of time it takes to make them. These bumpers are 5 inches high.

Materials

1½ yards 45-inch-wide fabric for 2 long and 2
  short bumpers to fit a portacrib
2 yards for a regular size crib
2-inch-thick foam

Directions

1. Measure the side of your crib and determine how long you want to make the side bumpers. Some bumpers only come down halfway from the top, others cover the entire length of the sides.
2. Determine if you want a bumper for the top and bottom ends, or just one bumper at the top. Measure across and subtract 4½ inches for the 2 side bumpers and fabric bulk.
3. Measure and cut each foam piece with a scissors.
4. Adding ¼ inch for seam allowance all around, cut 2 pieces of fabric for the front and back of each foam piece.
5. Cut 2 pieces of fabric 2½ × 5½ inches for the ends of each bumper.
6. Cut 2 strips of fabric 2½ × the measured length of each bumper for the top and bottom edges.
7. With right sides facing and raw edges aligned, join top, sides, and bottom pieces together.
8. With right sides facing and raw edges aligned, join the 2 short ends as shown in Figure 1.
9. Fold the fabric around the foam piece and pin the corner seams. Remove from the foam and stitch.
10. Fold the fabric around the foam once more and turn the long raw edges under. Slip-stitch opening closed.

Ties

1. Cut a strip of fabric ¾ inch × 25 inches for each bumper tie.
2. Fold the long raw edges under ⅛ inch and press. Fold short ends under and press. Fold fabric in half lengthwise, wrong sides facing.
3. Stitch down long edge and across both ends to close.
4. Fold each tie in half lengthwise and tack securely to each corner for tying to crib rungs.

Appliqué Bibs

Boutique bibs are quite expensive to buy but are easy and inexpensive to make. This is a wonderful gift, as it is practical as well as good-looking. Choose the design and colors that most appeal to you. Each appliqué is secured with a zigzag stitch and the Velcro closure makes it easy to secure around baby's neck.

Materials
½ yard fabric
scraps of fabric for the appliqués
thin quilt batting
thread to match appliqué fabrics
Velcro tab fastener
Scrap of black felt and black embroidery floss or
    waterproof marker for faces
white glue

Directions
The main pattern piece includes a ¼-inch seam allowance. Appliqué pieces do not require a seam allowance.
1. Begin by enlarging the bib pattern (see page 73).
2. Enlarge the neck piece in the same way.
3. Pin bib patterns to main fabric and cut 2 of each.
4. With right sides facing and raw edges aligned, join neck piece to bib fabric. Open seams and press. Repeat on the back.

To make appliqués
1. Trace each appliqué element from these pages. Use patterns to cut each piece from fabric.
2. Pin each appliqué piece in position on the front of the bib fabric and zigzag stitch around edges with matching thread.

To finish
1. Cut a piece of quilt batting slightly smaller than the bib all around.
2. With right sides facing and raw edges aligned, pin the front and back bib fabric together on top of the batting.
3. Stitch around, leaving a small opening for

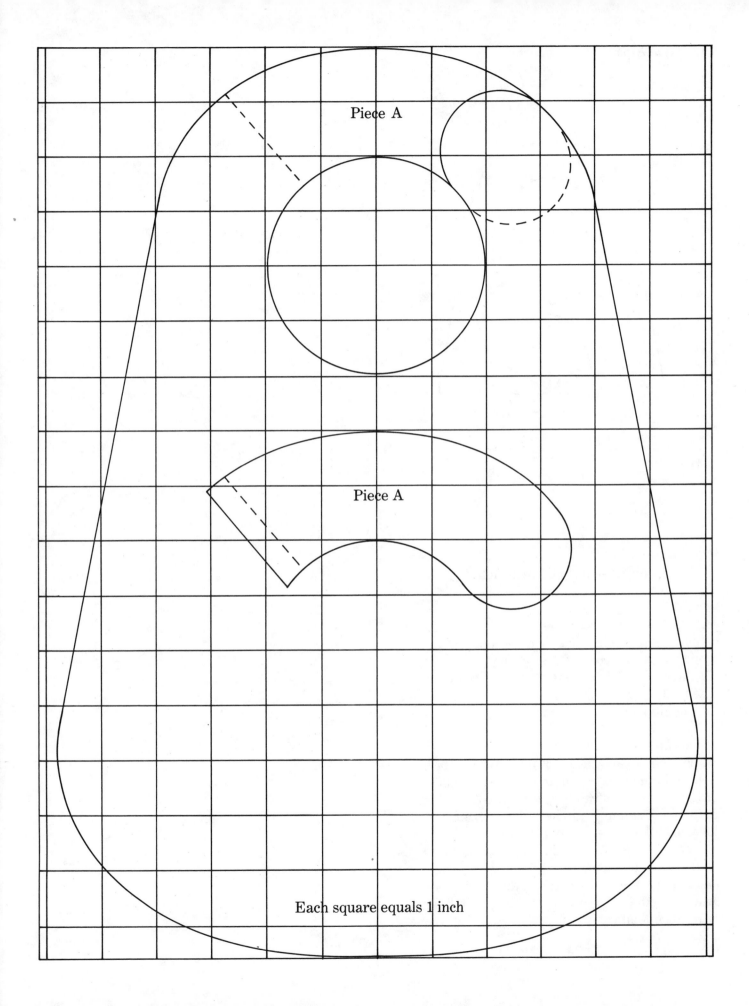

Piece A

Piece A

Each square equals 1 inch

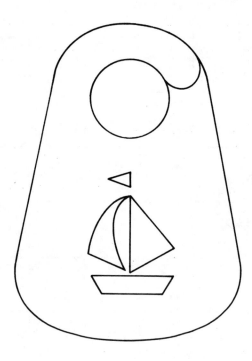

turning.

4. Trim around seams and turn right-side out.

5. Turn raw edges inside ¼ inch and slip-stitch closed.

6. Machine-stitch ¼ inch in from outside edge all around top of bib. (This can be done with contrasting thread color if desired.)

7. Attach a Velcro fastener to the underside of the neck piece and a corresponding tab to the top of the bib front.

To make details

1. For the bear's face, cut 3 tiny circles of black felt and glue in position for the eyes and nose.

2. Draw the mouth with waterproof marker, or take small running stitches with 2 strands of embroidery floss to stitch in position.

3. For the ducks, cut 3 tiny circles of felt for eyes and glue in position.

4. Using waterproof marker, draw wings on the ducks' bodies, or use a running stitch and 2 strands of embroidery floss.

Appliqué Bib patterns

Whimsical Pillow Toys

Make a group of soft animal toy pillows to accent any child's room. They are small and cuddly, perfect for an infant or toddler, and they are completely washable. Even a teenager would enjoy them on a bed, and I like to use them to add country charm to my den.

Materials (for animals)
Poly-Fil™ stuffing
scraps of black and white felt
tracing paper
stiff paper
white glue

Whale
¼ yard light blue calico
½ yard ¼-inch blue satin ribbon

Pig
¼ yard pink calico
½ yard ¼-inch pink satin ribbon

Elephant
¼ yard gray calico
1 yard ¼-inch rose satin ribbon

Cat
¼ yard light brown calico
scrap of dark brown calico
½ yard ¼-inch blue satin ribbon
2 tiny button eyes
small amount fusible webbing

Duck
small piece yellow calico
scrap of blue calico
scrap of red calico
½ yard ¼-inch yellow satin ribbon
small amount fusible webbing

Directions
All patterns include ¼-inch seam allowance. Trace all animal patterns and transfer to stiff paper for template (see page 14).

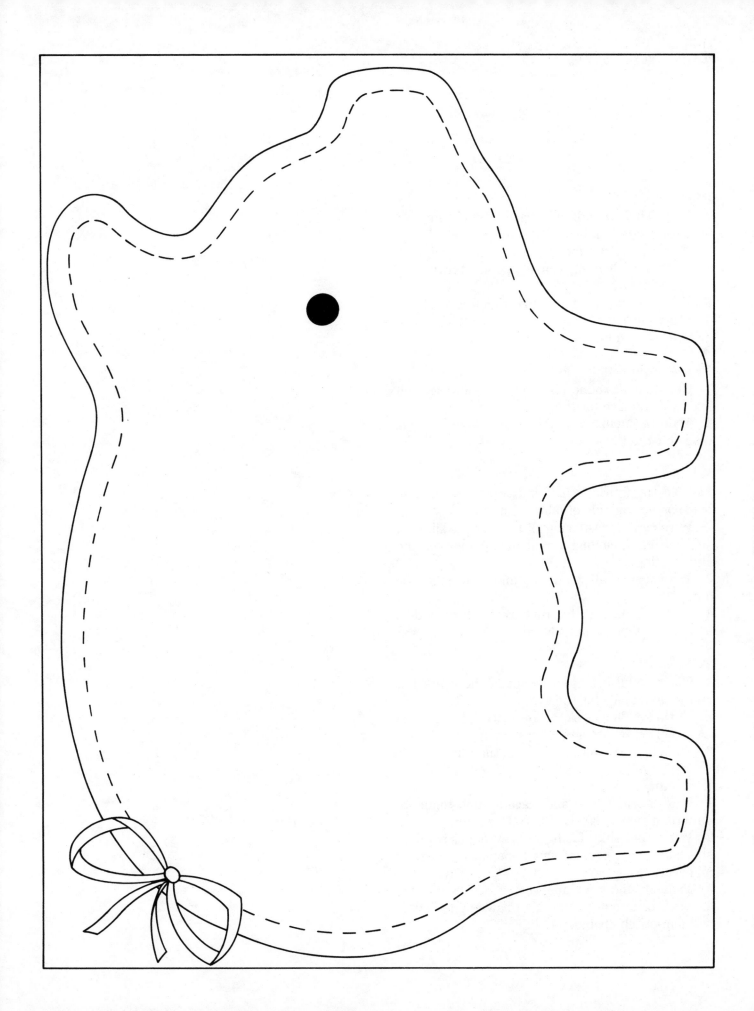

Pig

1. Fold fabric in half and trace around template on wrong side of fabric. Cut out.
2. With right sides facing and raw edges aligned, stitch around, leaving a small opening for turning and stuffing.
3. Trim around seam and turn right-side out.
4. Stuff pig tightly, fold raw edges under, and slip-stitch opening closed.

To finish

1. Cut a small round circle out of the black felt and glue in place for the eye.
2. Make a small pink ribbon bow and stitch in place for the tail.

Whale

1. Fold the fabric in half and trace around template on wrong side of fabric. Cut out.
2. With right sides facing and raw edges aligned, stitch around, leaving a small opening for turning and stuffing.
3. Trim around all seam lines and turn right-side out.
4. Stuff whale tightly, turn raw edges under, and slip-stitch opening closed.

To finish

1. Cut a small round circle out of the white felt and glue in place for the eye.
2. Cut a smaller circle of the black felt and glue on top of the white circle for the pupil.
3. Tie a blue ribbon bow around the tail.

Elephant

1. Fold fabric in half and trace around template on wrong side of fabric. Cut out.
2. With right sides facing and raw edges aligned, stitch around, leaving a small opening for turning and stuffing.
3. Trim around seam and turn right-side out.
4. Stuff elephant tightly, fold raw edges under, and slip-stitch opening closed.

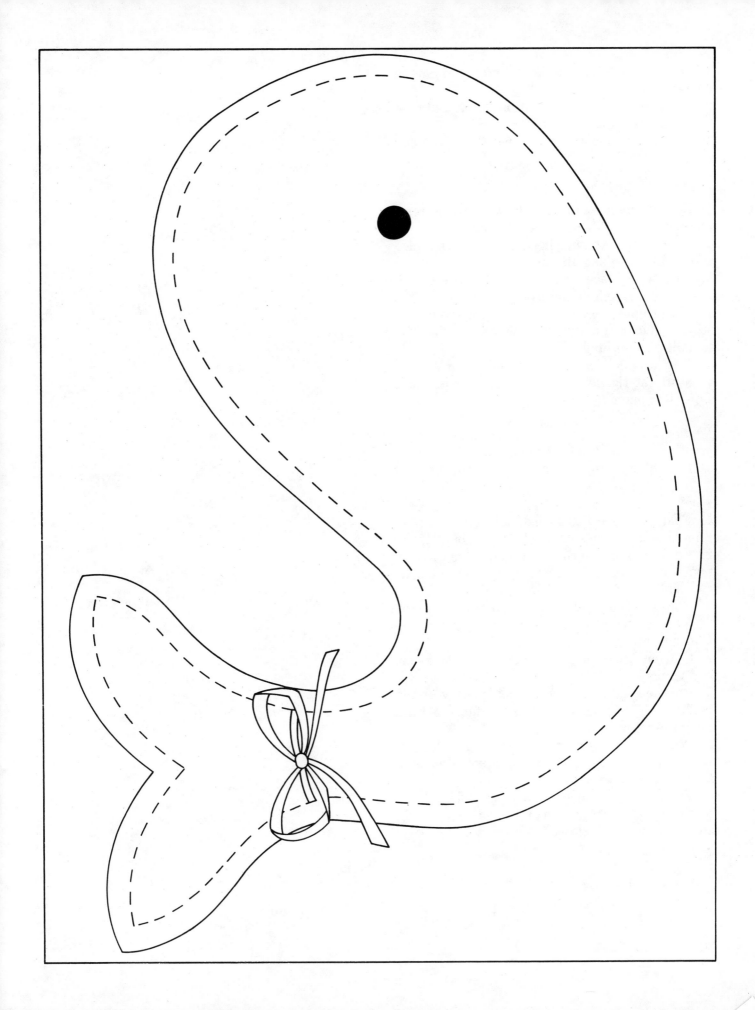

To finish

1. Cut a small circle out of white felt and glue in place for the eye.
2. Cut a smaller circle out of black felt and glue on top of the white circle for the pupil.
3. Tie a rose ribbon bow around the elephant's neck.

Cat

1. Fold the fabric in half and trace around template on wrong side of fabric. Cut out.
2. Trace tail pattern, pin to dark brown calico and fusible webbing and cut out.
3. Pin tail in place on front of cat. Fuse to the fabric with a medium-hot iron.
4. With right sides facing and raw edges aligned, stitch around the cat, leaving an opening for turning and stuffing.
5. Trim around seam and turn right-side out.
6. Stuff cat tightly, fold raw edges under, and slip-stitch opening closed.

To finish

1. Stitch tiny button eyes in place.
2. Tie a blue ribbon bow around the cat's neck.

Duck

1. Fold yellow calico in half and trace around template on wrong side of fabric. Cut out.
2. Fold the blue calico in half and trace the pattern for the head on the wrong side of the fabric. Cut out.
3. Fold the red calico in half and trace the pattern for the wing on the wrong side of the fabric. Cut out.
4. Cut out fusible webbing pieces for the heads and wings.
5. Pin the head and wing pieces in place with the fusible webbing between. Fuse to fabric with a medium-hot iron.
6. With right sides facing and raw edges aligned, stitch around the duck, leaving a small opening for turning and stuffing.
7. Trim around seams and turn right-side out.
8. Stuff duck tightly, fold raw edges under, and slip-stitch opening closed.

To finish

1. Cut a small circle out of the black felt and glue in place for the eye.
2. Tie a yellow ribbon bow around the cat's neck.

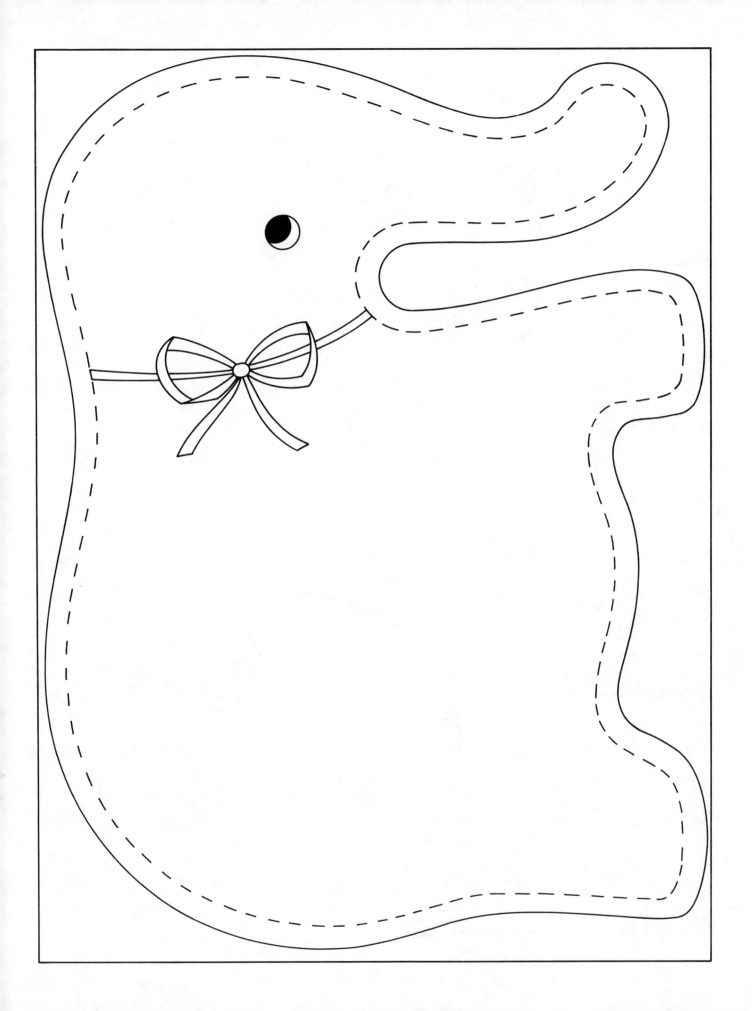

82

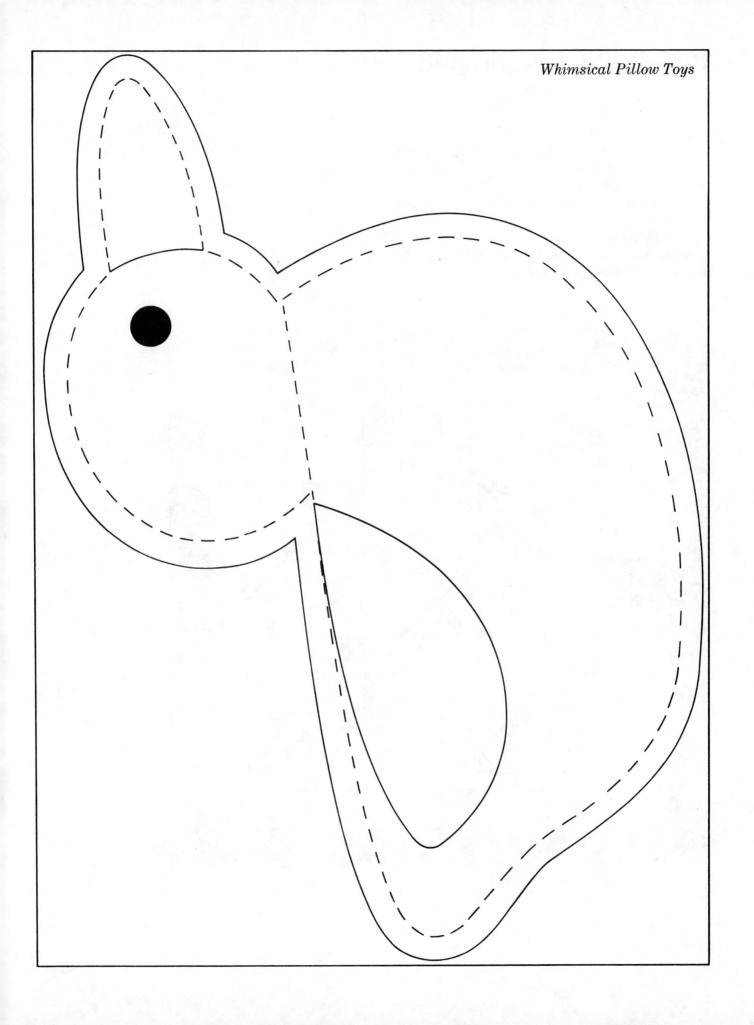

Pinwheel Carriage Quilt

We used calico with the same pattern in green with a white print and white with a green print for this carriage quilt. The pinwheel is a whimsical pattern for a baby's quilt, which is a quick and easy project.

The 42-inch-square size is good for a carriage, bassinet, or to carry along when you travel. This is also a good size for a wallhanging.

Materials
(All fabric is 45 inches wide.)
1¼ yards white calico
2¼ yards green calico (includes backing)
quilt batting

Directions
All fabric measurements for cutting include a ¼-inch seam allowance.

Cut the following:
green calico (borders)
    2 pieces 3½ × 42½ inches
    2 pieces 3½ × 36½ inches
(backing)
    1 square 42½ × 42½ inches
    1 piece 18 × 26 inches
    4 squares 3½ × 3½ inches
white calico (borders)
    2 pieces 3½ × 30½ inches
    1 piece 18 × 26 inches
    8 pieces 6½ × 9½ inches (A)
    6 squares 6½ × 6½ inches (B)
    2 pieces 3½ × 6½ inches (C)

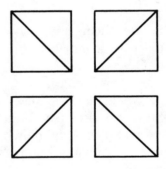

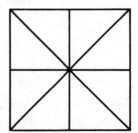

Figure 1   Make 11

Quick and Easy Triangle Method

1. On wrong side of white calico piece (18 × 26 inches) measure and mark 22 squares 4 × 4 inches.
2. Draw lines diagonally through all squares in the same direction.
3. With right sides facing and raw edges aligned, pin to same size piece of green calico.
4. Stitch ¼ inch on each side of all diagonal lines.
5. Cut on all solid lines. Open seams and press. You will have 44 squares of white and green calico triangles.

To make a block

1. With right sides facing and raw edges aligned, stitch 4 squares together to form a pinwheel pattern as shown in Figure 1. Make 11.
2. Open seams and press.

To make rows

1. With right sides facing and raw edges aligned, join one C piece to a pinwheel block along the long edge.
2. Next, join with an A piece.
3. Join to a pinwheel block, followed by a B piece and finally another B piece (see Figure 2).
4. Continue to join pieces and pinwheel blocks to create five rows as shown in Figure 2.
5. Open seams and press.

Joining rows

1. With right sides facing and raw edges aligned, join Row 1 to Row 2 along top edge.
2. Continue to join rows in this way. Open seams and press.

Borders

1. With right sides facing and raw edges aligned, join a green square (3½ × 3½ inches) to each short edge of white pieces (3½ × 30½ inches).
2. With right sides facing and raw edges aligned, join each strip to the top and bottom edges of the quilt top.

Outside border

1. With right sides facing and raw edges aligned, join green strips (3½ × 36½ inches) to the top and bottom edges of the quilt top.
2. Repeat with remaining side strips (3½ × 42½ inches). Open seams and press.

Quilting

1. Cut the batting ¼ inch smaller than the quilt top all around.
2. Baste the top, batting, and backing together with long stitches through all three layers. Begin at the center of the quilt and baste to each corner.
3. Using a small running stitch, quilt ¼ inch on each side of all seam lines. Quilt a grid pattern in the large white pieces and borders if desired (see page 17).

To finish

1. When all quilting is complete, remove all basting stitches.
2. Fold the raw edges under ¼ inch and press. Stitch together with a slip stitch.

Figure 2

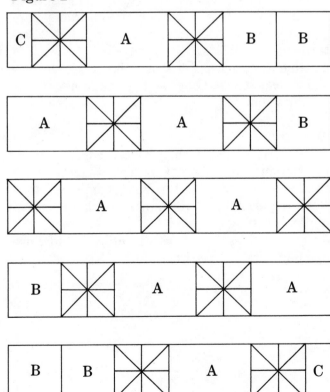

Stuffed Frog

Make a stuffed calico frog to sit in baby's crib or carriage. You can use any scrap of calico for the top and a solid for the underside. This toy measures 9 × 13 inches. It's a quick, easy, and inexpensive bazaar item that will sell quickly.

Materials
1 piece calico 10 × 14 inches
1 piece solid fabric 10 × 14 inches
Poly-Fil™ stuffing
scrap each of white, red, and black felt
white glue

Directions
1. Enlarge each of the pattern pieces (see page 13).
2. Pin top piece to calico fabric and cut 2 (1 in reverse).
3. Pin bottom piece on solid fabric and cut 1.
4. With right sides facing and raw edges aligned, join two top pieces along the curved long edge from point A to point B. Open seams and press.
5. Cut two large circles the size of a quarter from white felt. Cut two smaller circles (dime size) from black felt. Cut tongue from red felt. (Pattern shown full size.)
6. Glue the black felt onto the white felt as shown on pattern. Glue each eye on either side of center seam.

To finish
1. With right sides facing and raw edges aligned, pin top and underside of the frog together with the tongue between at the front seam.
2. Stitch around, leaving small opening for turning and stuffing.
3. Turn right-side out. Stuff until full and close opening with a slip-stitch.

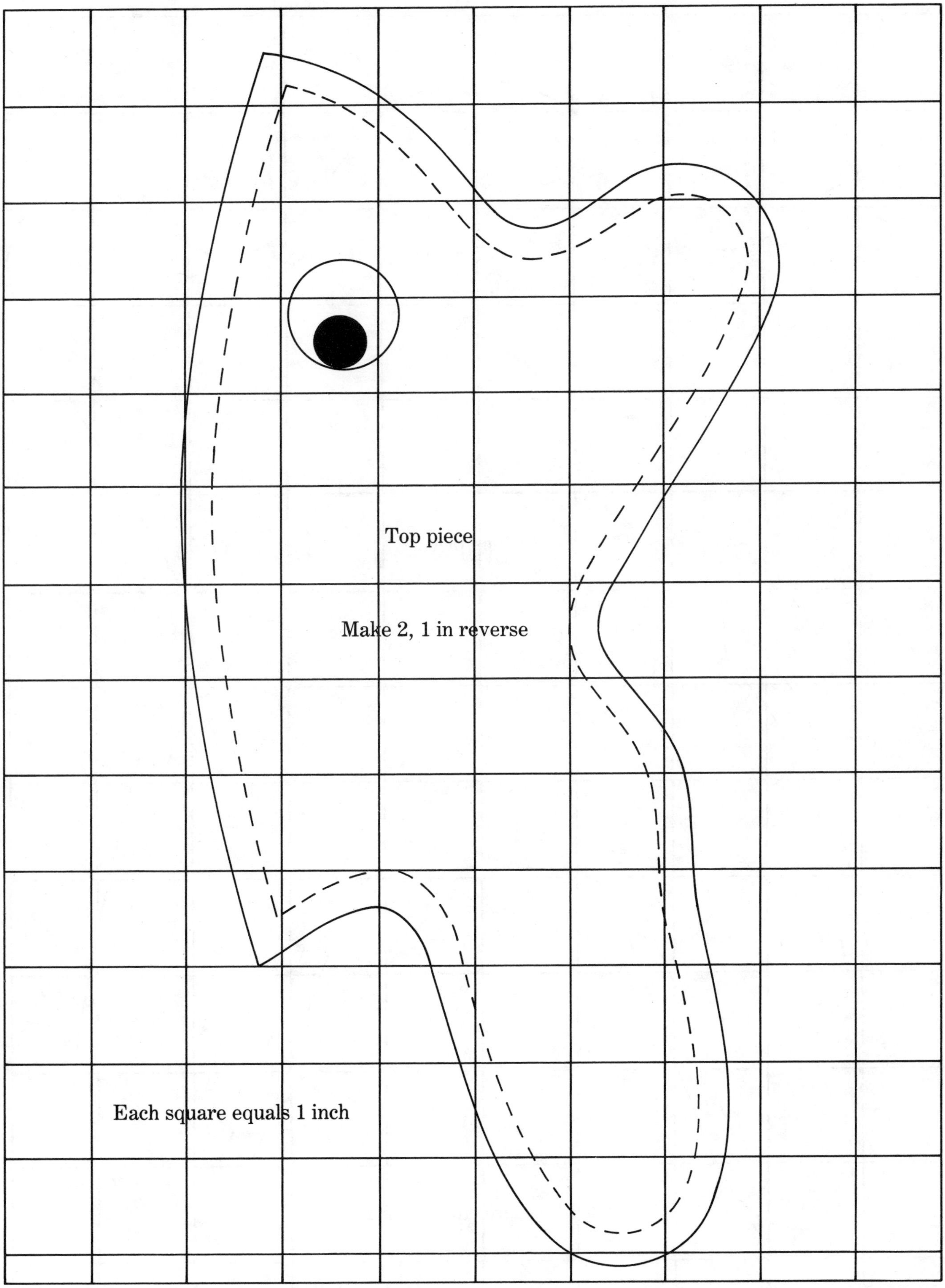

Top piece

Make 2, 1 in reverse

Each square equals 1 inch

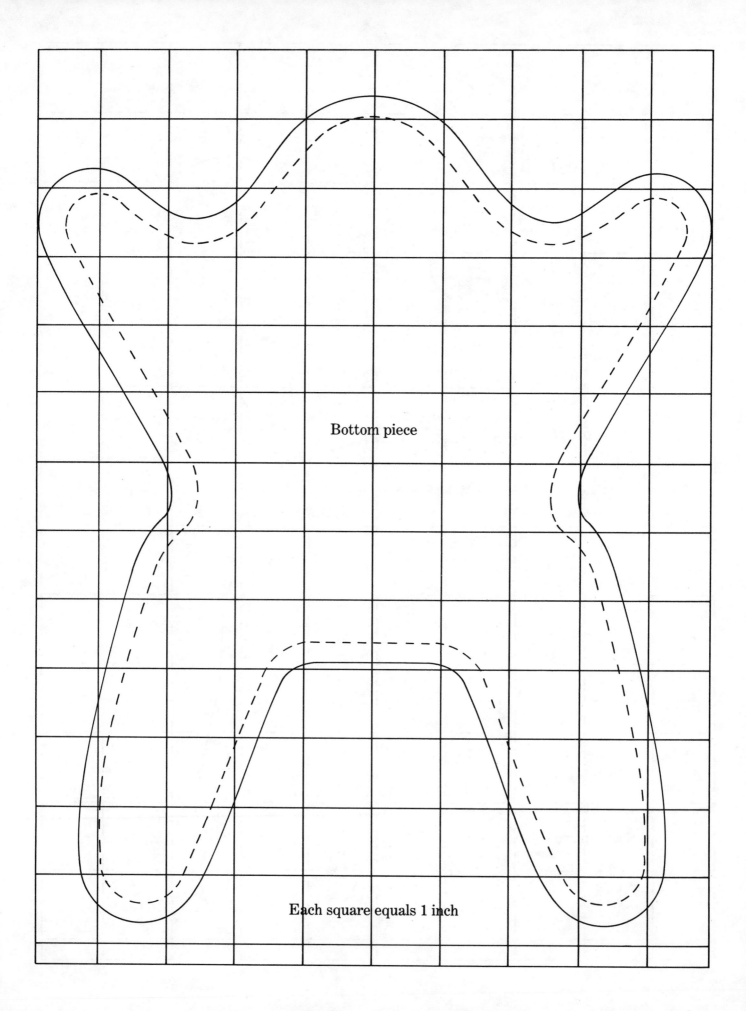

Bottom piece

Each square equals 1 inch

Patchwork Baby Jacket

This patchwork jacket is made from 3-inch fabric squares. You can use a light and dark print, as I've done here, or use scraps of different colors. I've made this project from flannel squares as well, and it is soft and warm to the touch. Use one of the fabrics for the lining. This jacket will fit an infant up to three months old. For 6- to 12-month size, cut the squares 4 × 4 inches.

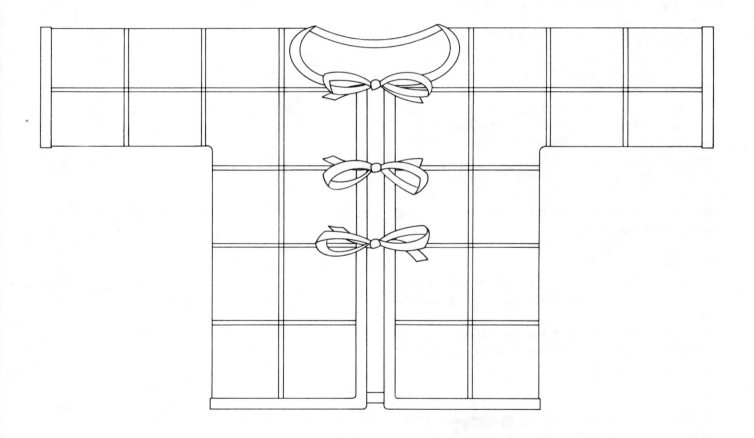

Materials

¼ yard white calico print
¼ yard aqua calico print
½ yard peach calico for lining
½ yard thin quilt batting

Directions

1. Cut 20 squares 3 × 3 inches from the light fabric.
2. Cut 20 squares 3 × 3 inches from the aqua fabric.
3. For the shoulders cut 4 pieces 3 × 4 inches from each of the fabrics.
4. Refer to Figure 1 for placement. With right sides facing and raw edges aligned, join a light and dark square along one side, leaving a ¼-inch seam allowance. Open seams and press.
5. Make 3 more sets of 2 squares each in this way.
6. With right sides facing and raw edges aligned, join all squares together so you have 4 rows of 2. Repeat for opposite side of front of jacket.
7. Continue to join all squares as indicated on the diagram, making sure to place the 8 larger pieces across the middle of the arm and neck section.
8. You now have a patchwork cross. Place this on your lining fabric and cut out the entire shape. Cut a 10-inch slit up the middle of the front of the lining.
9. Cut an oval from both fabrics for neck opening as indicated on the diagram.

To quilt

1. Remove the patchwork top piece and use this as a pattern to cut a batting piece. Trim batting slightly all around.
2. Pin the patchwork piece to the batting and machine-stitch along all seam lines on front of jacket.

To finish

1. With right sides facing and raw edges aligned, stitch the back side seams to the front side seams, continuing along the sleeve and under-arms. Turn right-side out and press.
2. Repeat for lining but do not turn. Press.
3. Slip lining inside top piece and adjust so sleeve edges and front opening line up. Pin together.
4. Turn raw edges of front and lining to the inside and press. Pin together.

5. Cut a bias strip of aqua calico $1 \times 16\frac{1}{2}$ inches. Turn raw edges under $\frac{1}{4}$ inch and press. With wrong sides facing, fold strip in half lengthwise and press.

6. Use this strip to bind neck edges. Slip-stitch all around.

7. Cut 6 strips 1×8 inches from lining fabric for front ties. Turn raw edges under $\frac{1}{4}$ inch, fold in half and stitch along open edge.

8. Position ties on jacket front and pin between top and lining. Slip-stitch around all open edges of the jacket to finish.

Figure 1

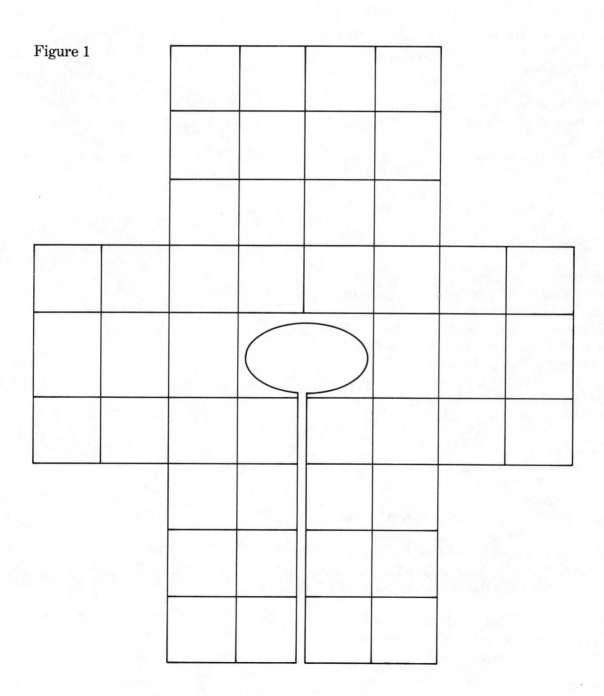

Patchwork Teddy Bear

Make your own country bear from 1½-inch square patchwork fabric. You simply piece the squares to create the fabric from which you cut out the teddy bear pattern pieces. You can make it with faded pastels as I did here, or using a bold red or blue color with muslin. It's easy and fun to make this 24-inch stuffed toy.

Materials
scraps of muslin and a variety of calico to make approximately 360 2-inch squares
Poly-Fil™ stuffing
tracing paper
4 flat buttons approximately the size of a nickel
small scraps of black felt or black embroidery floss
carpet thread or heavy thread

Directions
All pattern pieces include ¼-inch seam allowance.
1. Cut scraps of calico and muslin into 2-inch squares.
2. With right sides facing, stitch a muslin square to a calico square along one edge. See page 19 for quick and easy sewing method.
3. Stitch the squares together in rows of 10 across and 9 down to create a patchwork fabric. Make 4 pieces of 90 squares each.
4. Enlarge the teddy bear pattern pieces (see page 13) and pin each one to the patchwork fabric. Cut out.

Head and face
1. With right sides facing, pin the head gusset between the 2 head pieces to that it falls between the nose and back of the neck.
2. Stitch both seams. Next, stitch from tip of nose to edge of neck front. Turn right-side out.
3. Cut 2 black circles (about the size of a dime) from felt and glue or tack in position on each seam line, approximately 3 inches from tip of nose.
4. Cut a black triangle for the nose and tack or glue in position. For mouth, use embroidery floss and take running stitches from the center of the

94

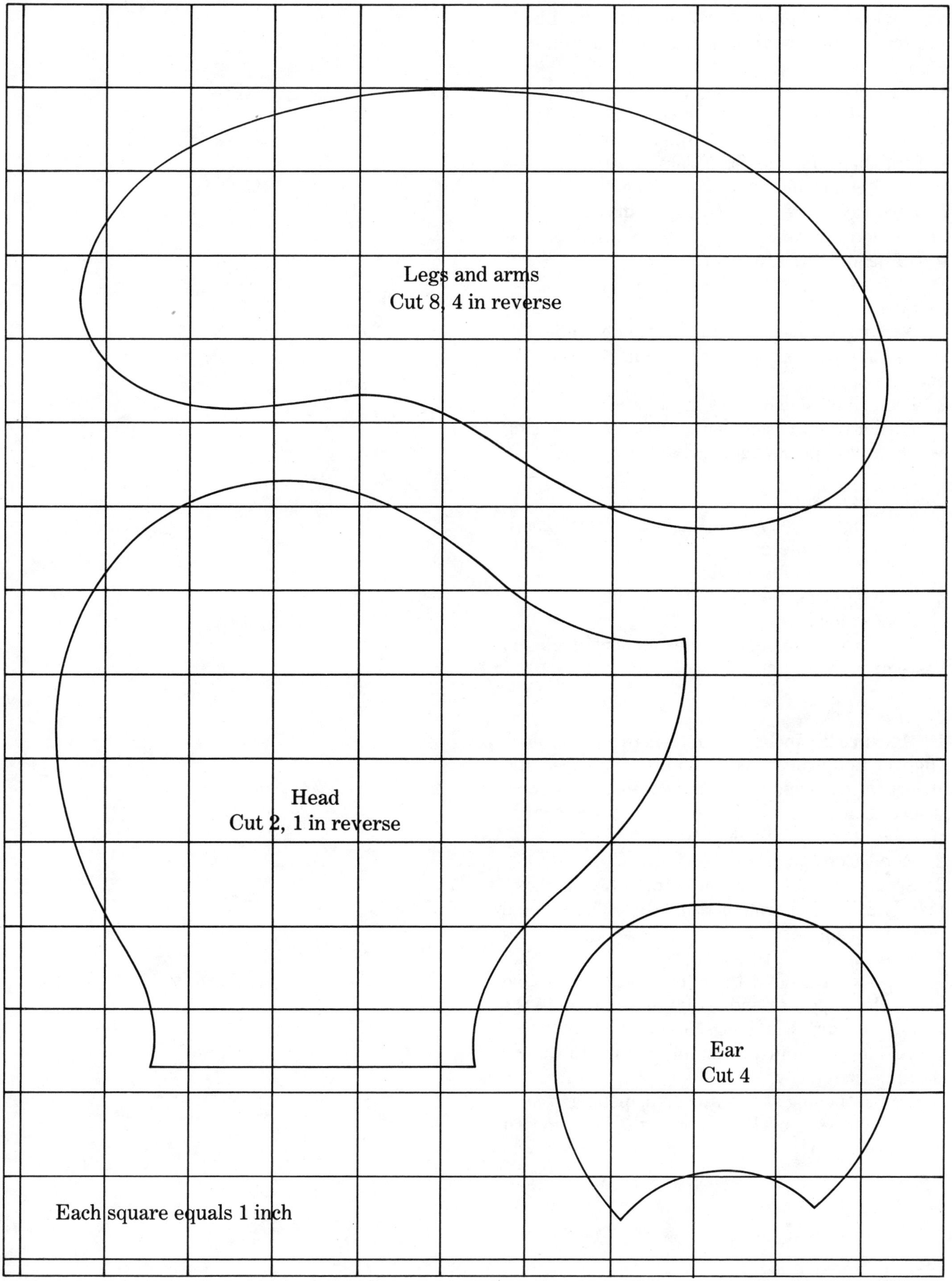

Legs and arms
Cut 8, 4 in reverse

Head
Cut 2, 1 in reverse

Ear
Cut 4

Each square equals 1 inch

bottom of the triangle down 1 inch. Stitch a 1 inch line across the bottom of this vertical line running from the nose.

5. With right sides facing, pin 2 ear pieces together and stitch around the curved edge, leaving straight edge open. Turn to right side.

6. Stuff head firmly. Stuff ears and run a gathering stitch around open edge of each ear.

7. Turn raw edges of each ear to inside and pin in position approximately 3 inches apart on the top of head. Stitch to secure.

Body

1. With right sides facing and raw edges aligned, stitch body pieces together, leaving the top edge open for turning.

2. Turn right-side out but do not stuff.

3. Turn raw edges under and run a gathering stitch around neck edge. Leave loose for now.

Arms and legs

1. With right sides facing and raw edges aligned, stitch the arm pieces together, leaving the wide curved end open for stuffing.

2. Turn right-side out and stuff ¾ full.

3. Repeat for legs.

4. Turn raw edges of openings under ¼ inch and baste around.

To finish

1. Measure 2½ inches down from the side of neck edge of body and secure 1 button inside body. Insert a corresponding button inside an arm where it attaches to the body and stitch arm to the body through the buttons.

2. Repeat on the other side.

3. Secure each leg in the same way approximately 2½ inches from bottom edge. They should be in a sitting position.

4. Stuff body so it is firmly packed.

5. Slip-stitch around the curve of each arm and leg to close opening and secure more firmly to the body. The arms and legs are not meant to be moveable. The buttons simply secure the limbs more permanently.

6. Pull gathering stitches around opening of head and stitch to the neck opening of the body so that it is securely in place.

Each square equals 1 inch

Head gusset

Place on fold

Body
Cut 2

For Gifts

Clutch Purse

Pick a delicate floral, overall print for a clutch purse or lingerie case. The finished size is 9 × 13 inches, which is nice and roomy. The lining is a bright, contrasting solid color. The blue lines on the fabric are the stitches that accent and quilt the fabric. Originally, hand embroidery was often used as a quilting technique when a decorative finish was preferred.

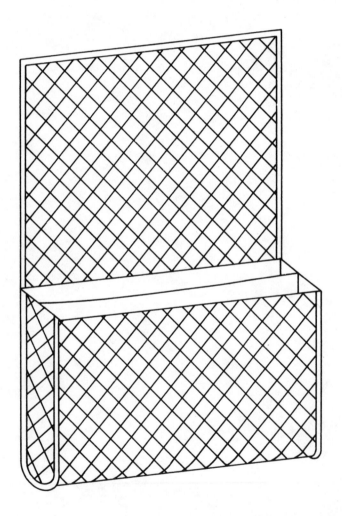

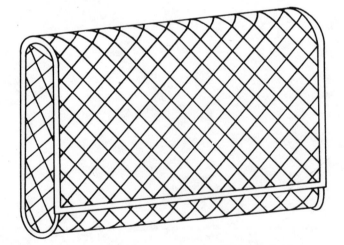

Materials

½ yard 45-inch-wide printed fabric
½ yard (any width) solid fabric
quilt batting
thread to match fabric
needle
tracing paper
ruler
hard pencil
button or snap for closure

Directions

All directions include a ¼-inch seam allowance.

1. Begin by tracing pattern piece A. This is the pattern for the sides of the bag.

2. Pin the pattern to the printed fabric and cut two. Repeat for lining fabric.

3. From the printed fabric, cut pieces in the following sizes:

    14 × 27½ inches for main piece
    10½ × 14 inches for flap lining

4. From solid fabric, cut pieces in the following sizes:

    7½ × 12¾ inches for pocket
    12¾ × 16 inches for main lining piece

5. Cut batting 14 × 27½ inches.

6. Cut 2 pieces of batting, using pattern piece A as a guide. Cut away seam allowance.

To quilt

1. Use a ruler to mark off a grid over the main fabric piece (14 × 27½ inches).

2. Pin batting to the back of the main piece and machine-stitch along all drawn lines, stopping ¼ inch from the fabric's edge.

3. Rule off lines on the flap lining fabric and machine-stitch without batting.

4. Rule off lines on the side pieces (A) and pin to the corresponding batting pieces.

5. Stitch along all marked lines.

To assemble

1. Place the main fabric piece right-side up, lengthwise, on your work table.

2. With right sides facing and raw edges aligned,

pin the flap lining piece to one short end of the main piece.

3. Stitch around the 3 outside edges. Clip corners.

4. Clip around the curve of the side pieces (A) in the seam allowance.

5. Place the curved piece face down on the edge of the short end of the fabric, with the curve in the center of the main piece, and pin along the outside edge.

6. Fold the right-hand edge of the main piece forward and continue to pin the curve of the side piece and the long edge, with right sides facing. Repeat on the opposite edge to set side pieces (A) in place. Stitch around.

7. Turn the lining and main section to the right side and press.

Lining

1. With right side up, pin the pocket piece to the front of the lining, ½ inch from one short end.

2. With right sides facing and raw edges aligned, join the side pieces (A) as for the outside, with the pocket piece between, at the seam line. Stitch across the bottom edge of the pocket.

3. Turn top edge of the lining ¼ inch to the wrong side of the fabric and press. Turn raw edge of main bag piece to the inside ¼ inch and press.

4. Slip lining into the bag and slip-stitch around the top edges to join the outside and the lining and to hide the raw edge of the inside flap.

To finish

Stitch ½ inch from the edge around the outer edge of the flap. Pin the sides and outer bag together ½ inch in from the seam line. Stitch around the outside curved piece (A) for a finished, quilted edge.

Place a snap closure on the inside, center edge of the flap. Fold forward and place the corresponding snap piece on the bag. You can also use a button with a loop closing or a piece of Velcro fastening tape in place of the snap.

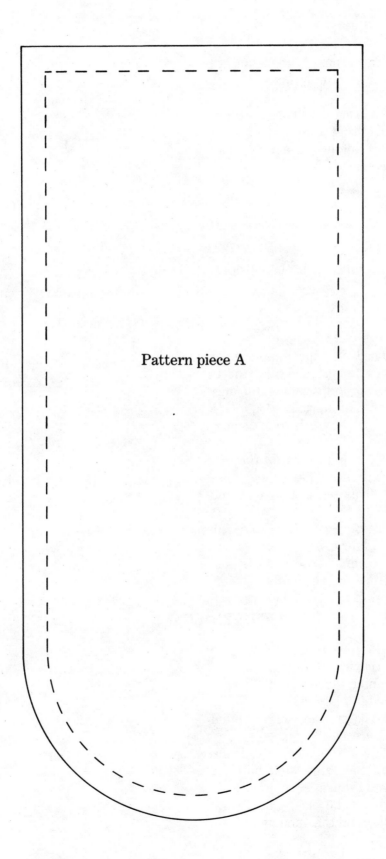

Pattern piece A

Tissue Box Cover

A small project like this is easy to make for gift giving, bazaar sales, or to pretty up your own bath or bedroom.

An overall small print is a good choice for quilting in a grid pattern. Quilting is an option, but it makes the project more elegant. Use a contrasting piping for added interest.

Materials
¼ yard calico fabric
thin quilt batting
1 yard piping in color to match
embroidery floss to match a color in the fabric
quilting needle
tissue box

Directions
The tissue box is used as your template for measuring fabric pieces. You can use these directions for making a cover for any size box, the only variable being the amount of fabric used.
1. Begin by cutting 1 piece of fabric to fit the top of the box, adding ½ inch all around.
2. Measure the perimeter and height of the box and cut 1 strip of fabric to these dimensions, adding ½ inch all around. This piece wraps around the four sides of the box.
3. Cut a piece of batting ½ inch smaller all around for each piece of fabric.
4. If there are no guidelines, such as stripes, checks, or a grid pattern on your fabric print, rule off evenly spaced horizontal and vertical lines, using a ruler and hard pencil or water soluble marker.
5. Pin the corresponding batting piece to the wrong side of each fabric piece.
6. Remove the top opening piece from the tissue box. Using this as your template, center it on the top fabric piece with the batting and mark around it with a pencil (see Figure 1).
7. Working ½ inch inside the lines you just drew, cut out an opening on the fabric and batting. Notch curved edges (see Figure 2).
8. Cut a piece of fabric on the bias, 1 inch wide and long enough to fit around the opening plus an

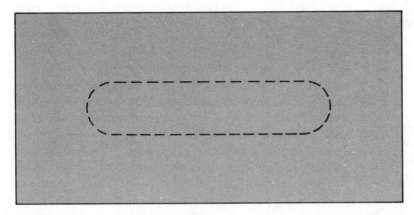

Figure 1

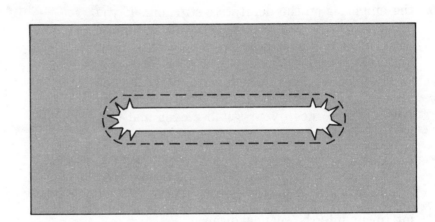

Figure 2

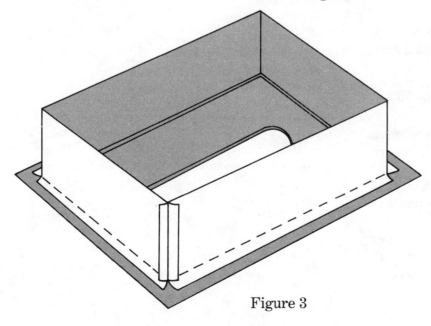

Figure 3

105

extra ½ inch. Turn the long edges under ¼ inch and press. Turn 1 short end under ½ inch and press. Fold the strip in half lengthwise and press.
9. Encase the raw edge of the opening in the bias strip, overlapping the edges where they meet. Stitch around.

To quilt

Using embroidery thread in a contrasting or matching color, separate all 6 strands. Using 3 strands only, quilt along the premarked lines, using a back or running stitch (see page 22). An alternative way to quilt the fabric is on the machine, using a matching thread on the fabric. In this way you will have a quilted project without the emphasis on the decorative stitching. If you enjoy lap work you can simply quilt the fabric with small running stitches as one might do for a quilt (see page 17).
1. Begin on the back of each panel. Make a small knot and pull the thread through the batting and fabric. Try to keep your stitches even and taut without bunching the fabric as you sew.
2. If stitching on the machine, set the stitch-length dial for a longer stitch than the one you would use for regular seam stitching, but not as loose as for a basting stitch. Do not allow stitching to run into the seam allowance.

To assemble

1. With right sides facing and raw edges aligned, join the short ends of the side piece, leaving a ½-inch seam allowance.
2. With raw edges aligned, pin the piping around the outer edge of the top piece of fabric. Stitch around.
3. With right sides facing and piping between, pin and join the top and side sections (see Figure 3).
4. Trim all seam allowances as close to the stitching line as possible. Turn right-side out and slip over the tissue box.
5. Pull the cover down so it fits comfortably over the box and turn the raw edge under ¼ inch all around the bottom of the cover. Pin in place.
6. Remove the cover and stitch around the bottom edge. Replace on the tissue box.

Eyeglass Case

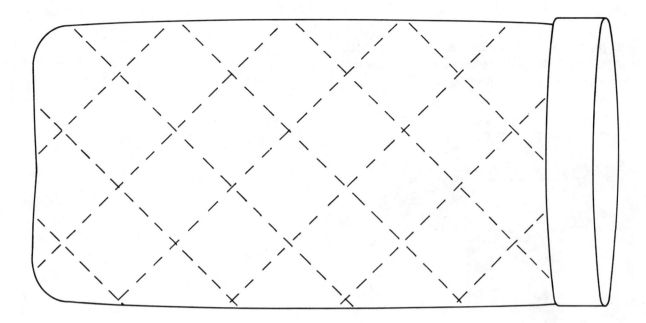

This tiny, overall, delicate rosebud print is perfect for an eyeglass case. The lines are done with embroidery stitches in order to quilt the fabric and add this delightful decorative touch. The craftwork was executed by the talented Kate Rumsey.

Materials
7 × 14½ inches delicate print fabric
7 × 14½ inches solid fabric (bright red used here)
7 inches decorative braid (green)
6½ × 14 inches thin quilt batting
1 skein embroidery floss (red)
embroidery needle

Directions
1. Cut printed outside fabric and solid lining in half so you have 4 pieces of fabric, 3½ × 7¼ inches each.
2. Cut batting in half so you have 2 pieces 6¼ × 7 inches.
3. Pin both outside fabric pieces to the batting pieces.
4. Draw a grid across the fabric, between the floral pattern, using a light pencil.
5. Using 3 strands of the embroidery floss, take small running stitches along all marked lines through the fabric and batting on both pieces of fabric.
6. With right sides facing, stitch front and back quilted fabric together along side and bottom edges, leaving the top edge open. Turn.

Lining
1. With right sides facing and raw edges aligned, stitch the 2 lining pieces together with ⅜-inch seam allowance along the side and bottom edges. Leave the top edge open. (The lining should be slightly smaller in order to fit comfortably inside the case.)
2. Trim seams and clip corners, but do not turn right-side out.
3. Slip the lining inside the quilted case and smooth into position.
4. Make sure that the side seams line up and tack the lining in position at the bottom corners.

To finish
1. Turn the top raw edges of the outside case and the lining ¼ inch to the inside (between outside and lining) and press.
2. Pin the decorative braid or ribbon around the top edge.
3. Slip-stitch braid and top edge of fabric and lining all around. Slip-stitch bottom edge of braid to top fabric only.

Shoo-Fly Pillows

Each pillow is 15 × 15 inches and made with similar colors, but not the exact fabrics. This design is easy to make and quilt for a lasting gift.

Materials
½ yard blue calico (A)
½ yard peach calico (B)
¼ yard white fabric (C)
quilt batting (¼ yard for 2 pillows)
Poly-Fil™ stuffing
62 inches blue piping

Directions
All measurements for cutting fabric include a ¼-inch seam allowance.

Cut the following:
blue calico (A)
    2 squares 6 × 6 inches—cut into 2 triangles
        each
    1 square 5½ × 5½ inches
peach calico (B)
    2 squares 6 × 6 inches—cut into 2 triangles
        each
    4 rectangles 3 × 5½ inches

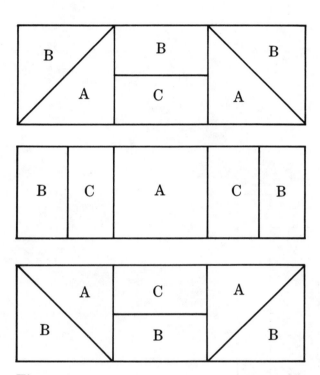

Figure 1

1 square 15½ × 15½ inches (backing)
white (C)
    4 rectangles 3 × 5½ inches

To make block
1. With right sides facing and raw edges aligned, join a B triangle to an A triangle along the diagonal to make a square 5½ × 5½ inches. Make four.
2. Join a B rectangle with a C rectangle in the same way. Open seams and press.

To make rows
1. With right sides facing and raw edges aligned, join 3 squares together to make a row as shown in Figure 1.
2. Continue to make rows of 3 squares each in the same way.

To join rows
1. With right sides facing and raw edges aligned, join Row 1 to Row 2. Open seams and press.
2. Continue to join Row 2 to Row 3 in the same way.

Quilting
1. Cut batting piece ¼ inch smaller than pillow top. Pin pillow top to batting all around.
2. Using small running stitches, quilt ¼ inch on each side of all seam lines.

To finish
1. With right sides facing and raw edges aligned, pin the piping to pillow top. Stitch all around. For same fabric covered piping see page 23.
2. With right sides facing, pin pillow top to backing piece with the piping between. Stitch around 3 sides and 4 corners, using stitching from piping as a guide.
3. Trim seams, clip corners, and turn right-side out.
4. Stuff pillow. Turn raw edges under and slipstitch closed.

To make a second pillow, switch color A and B and follow the same directions as above.

Heart Wallhanging

This charming country wallhanging was made by Susan Fernald Joyce and is reminiscent of those found in early American homes. The unconventional placement of each appliqué, the embroidery stitches, and the hand quilting make this wallhanging project extra special. The finished size is 29 inches square and is perfect for a hallway, child's room, dining area—almost anywhere, to soften a room. Get out your scraps!

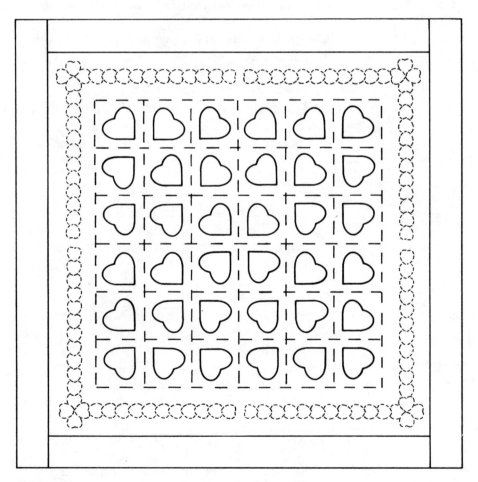

Figure 1

Materials

scraps of calicos in red, green, blue, and brown
1 yard muslin
½ yard navy blue calico for borders
1 yard backing fabric
29 × 29 inches thin quilt batting
wooden dowel, ½ inch in diameter, 31 inches long
nylon thread for hanging
tracing paper
stiff paper, such as oak tag, for template

Directions

The heart pattern includes a ¼-inch seam allowance.

1. Trace the heart pattern and transfer it to stiff paper to make the template (see page 14).
2. Using the template, draw around the outside edge on your scraps of calicos, using a variety of fabrics, and cut out 36 hearts.
3. Cut a piece of muslin 25½ × 25½ inches.
4. Leaving a 3-inch border all around, draw a square with a light pencil in the center of the muslin square.
5. Within this marked square, measure and mark off 3¼-inch squares, so you have 6 rows of 6 squares each (see Figure 1).

To make appliqués

1. Cut the seam allowance away from the template, making it ¼ inch smaller all around.
2. Place the heart template on the wrong side of each fabric heart. Cut into the seam allowance all around the fabric (see Figure 2).
3. With a medium-hot iron, turn the fabric edges over the edges of the template and press. Remove the template and repress the fabric edges down.
4. Pin a heart appliqué in each marked-off square on the muslin. The point of the heart should be placed in one corner of the square. Arrange each heart in a different direction (see Figure 3).
5. Stitch each heart appliqué in place with a slip stitch, overcast, or embroidered stitch (see page 22).
6. Trace and transfer the quilt design to the muslin border around the heart-filled square (see Fig-

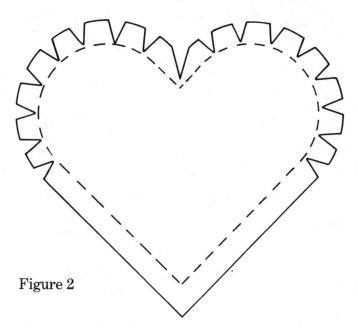

Figure 2

Clip seam allowance as shown for curved appliqué.

To make borders

1. From the navy blue calico cut the following:
    2 pieces 2½ × 25½ inches (sides)
    1 piece 2½ × 29½ inches (bottom)
    1 piece 4½ × 29½ inches (top)
2. With right sides facing and raw edges aligned, join the short side border strips to each edge of the heart fabric. Open seams and press.
3. With right sides facing and raw edges aligned, join the bottom strip to the bottom edge of the fabric. Open seams and press.
4. With right sides facing and raw edges aligned, join the top strip to the top edge of the fabric. Open seams and press. This piece will extend 2½ inches beyond the top and, when turned to the back, will become the channel for holding a hanging dowel.

Quilting

1. With wrong sides facing, baste the top, batting, and backing together.
2. Following your premarked quilting lines, take small running stitches through all three layers of fabric (see page 17). Do not quilt into the seam allowance.
3. When all quilting has been completed, remove the basting stitches.

To finish

1. Trim the batting ¼ inch all around.
2. Fold the raw edges of the fabric on the sides and bottom ¼ inch to the inside and slip-stitch all around.
3. Fold the top raw edge under ¼ inch and press.
4. Turn the top 2 inches of the border strip to the back to create a channel for the dowel. Press and slip-stitch to the backing fabric.
5. Insert dowel and hang with nylon thread if desired.

Note: Your quilted wallhanging can also be hung with Velcro fastening tape. Simply make the quilt border by cutting 2 pieces 2½ × 29½ inches for top and bottom. Finish as directed for bottom and side edges. Add a strip of Velcro tape to the top back edge of the quilt with corresponding Velcro tape on the wall.

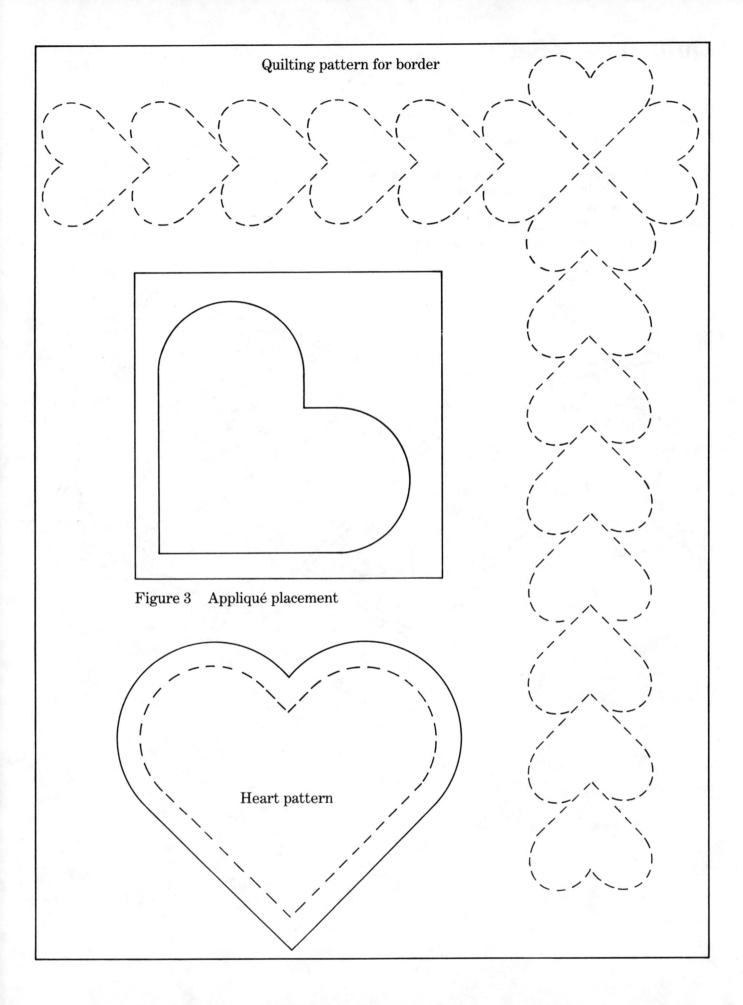

Quilting pattern for border

Figure 3   Appliqué placement

Heart pattern

Quilted Desk Set

I chose these handsome colors of wine, light gray, and dark gray calico to make a desk set for a man or woman. Each book cover and the fabric bow basket are quilted with a simple grid pattern that gives the projects dimension. One of the projects is a cover for a paperback book, which is a nice way to turn an inexpensive item into a gift.

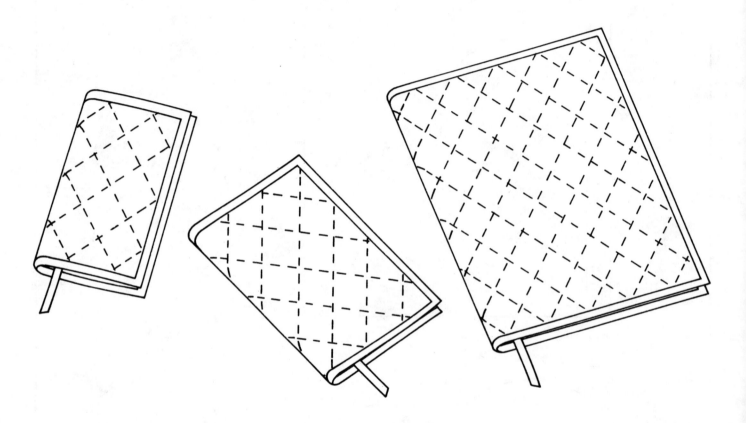

Materials

enough fabric to wrap a phone book, paperback,
  address book, or *TV Guide* plus 6 inches all
  around
same amount of fabric for lining
1-inch strips of contrasting fabric for borders
thin quilt batting to wrap around object
tissue box for bow basket

Paperback or *T V Guide* cover

1. Measure front, back, and spine and cut 1 piece
of fabric to size of this combined measurement.
Cut a piece of batting same size.
2. Cut lining fabric ¾ inch larger all around.
3. Cut 2 strips of lining fabric 1½ inches wide ×
length of the book plus 1 inch.
4. Cut another strip from the lining fabric, 1½ ×
9 inches.

Quilting

1. Using a light pencil and a ruler, draw a 1-inch
grid in a diamond pattern across the top fabric.
2. Center the batting on the wrong side of the
lining and place the top fabric over the batting.
There will be ¾ inch of lining all around. Pin the
3 layers together.
3. Take small running stitches along all marked
lines on the top fabric through all three layers.

To finish

1. Turn raw edges of the lining forward ¼ inch
and press.
2. Bring the lining fabric forward to cover the
top fabric to create a ½-inch border all around.
Slip-stitch to top fabric.
3. Fold each fabric strip in half lengthwise with
wrong sides facing. Turn raw edges under and
press.
4. Stitch down long edge and across ends.
5. Measure 2 inches in from each end on the lining and tack a strip in position to hold the cover
of the book.
6. Tack the third strip at the top edge of one side
of the lining to use as the bookmark.

Telephone Book Cover
1. Measure front, back, and spine and add 4½ inches to the width measurement. Cut 1 piece from top fabric.
2. Cut lining fabric same size. Cut quilt batting same size.
3. Cut contrasting fabric strips 1½ inches × width of fabric top, minus the extra 4½ inches, for top and bottom borders.
4. Cut 2 side border strips, 1½ inches × length of book.

Quilting
1. Using a light pencil or water soluble pen (or chalk on dark fabric), draw a 1¼-inch diamond grid across the top fabric.
2. Pin top, batting, and lining together and take small running stitches through all 3 layers along marked lines. Do not quilt into seam allowance all around.

To finish
1. Turn the raw edges of the short ends inside ¼ inch and press.
2. Machine- or slip-stitch these turned ends only.
3. Fold 2 inches of fabric on each end to the inside and press. These will become the flaps to hold the book cover.
4. Turn the raw edges of the fabric strips under ¼ inch and press.
5. With wrong sides facing and edges aligned, fold the strips in half lengthwise and press. Fit the top and bottom strips over the long raw edges of the fabric cover so you have a ½-inch border on front and back. Slip-stitch in position.
6. Repeat on each end where the fabric folds to create the flaps.
7. Add a bookmark strip as you did for the paperback cover if desired.

Bow Basket
1. Cut the top off a tissue box. Slit the corners and unfold, so it is a flat piece of cardboard (see Figure 1).
2. Cut a rectangle of lining fabric ¼ inch larger all around than the width and length of the box

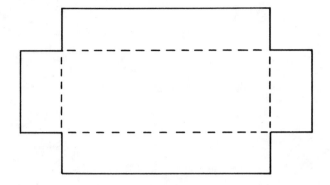

Figure 1   Flatten box

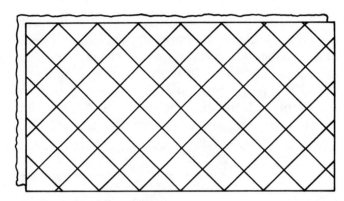

Figure 2   Quilted fabric

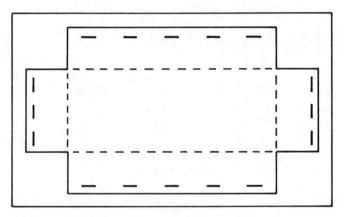

Figure 3   Box stapled to fabric

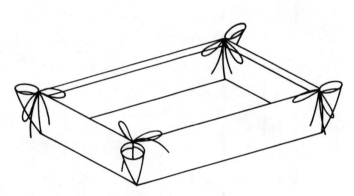

Bow basket

at the widest and longest points.

3. Cut quilt batting same size as lining piece.

4. Draw a 1-inch grid pattern on the lining fabric and pin to the batting.

5. Quilt along marked lines with small, even running stitches (see Figure 2).

6. Staple the lining and batting to one side of the box at the edges. Trim fabric and batting close to box edges, but *do not cut out* corners.

7. Cut front fabric ¾ inch larger than fabric on box all around.

8. Press edges under ¼ inch. With wrong sides facing, place lining, batting, and box on top of fabric (see Figure 3).

9. Bring edges of top fabric over to lining so there is a ½-inch border all around on the lining.

10. For ribbon ties, cut 8 strips ¾ × 7½ inches from lining fabric.

11. Turn raw edges under, fold in half lengthwise, and stitch along long edge. Tack each tie to the lining at each edge of the cardboard (approximately 2½ inches from each corner).

12. Fold the sides of the box up and tie the bows at each corner.

Schoolhouse Pillow

This traditional design is a favorite with quilt makers. It has been faithfully copied, revised, and translated in a variety of colors and sizes and adapts nicely to wallhangings, quilts, and pillows. The red, white, and blue colors used here by Peter Peluso, Jr., are bold and bright and create a contemporary look for this project. The finished pillow is 16 by 16 inches.

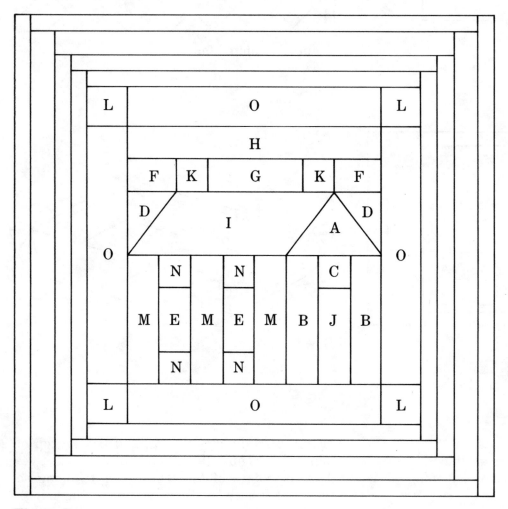

Figure 3

Materials

small amounts of the following: light blue calico;
    maroon, red, and white fabrics
¼ yard navy blue fabric
½ yard navy blue calico
2 yards navy blue piping
16-inch pillow form
tracing paper

Directions

All patterns and fabric measurements for cutting
include a ¼-inch seam allowance.

Trace the pattern pieces A, D, and I, which
are shown full size. These are the roof pieces. All
other pieces are squares or strips that can be
measured and cut from the fabric without a pattern.

Cut the following:
red fabric (borders)
    2 pieces 1 × 11 inches
    2 pieces 1 × 12 inches
    1 roof piece (A)
    2 roof pieces 1½ × 4½ inches (B)
    1 square 1½ × 1½ inches (C)
white fabric (borders)
    2 pieces 1 × 12 inches
    2 pieces 1 × 13 inches
    2 roof pieces (D)
    2 pieces 1½ × 2½ inches (E)
    2 pieces 1½ × 2 inches (F)
    1 piece 1½ × 3½ inches (G)
    1 piece 1½ × 8½ inches (H)
navy blue calico (border)
    2 pieces 1¾ × 13 inches
    2 pieces 1¾ × 15½ inches
    1 square 16½ × 16½ inches (backing)
    1 piece (I)
navy blue solid (borders)
    2 pieces 1 × 15½ inches
    2 pieces 1 × 16½ inches
    1 piece 1½ × 3½ inches (J)
    2 pieces 1½ × 1½ inches (K)
    4 squares 1¾ × 1¾ inches (L)

maroon
  3 pieces 1½ × 4½ inches (M)
  4 squares 1½ × 1½ inches (N)
light blue calico
  4 pieces 1¾ × 8½ inches (O)

To make top half of house block
1. With right sides facing and raw edges aligned, join D to I to A to D, as shown in Figure 1, Section 3.
2. With right sides facing and raw edges aligned, join F to K to G to K, followed by another F, as shown in Figure 1, Section 2.
3. With right sides facing and raw edges aligned, join the H piece to the Section 2 piece, then join Section 2 piece to Section 3 piece. Open all seams and press.

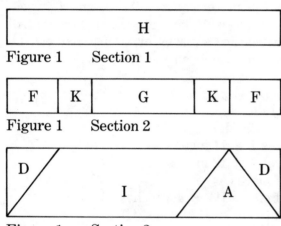

Figure 1   Section 1

Figure 1   Section 2

Figure 1   Section 3

To make bottom half of house block
1. With right sides facing and raw edges aligned, join N pieces to the short ends of E piece. Make 2.
2. Join C piece to short end of J piece. Open seams and press.
3. With right sides facing and raw edges aligned, join the pieces together as shown in Figure 2.

Figure 2

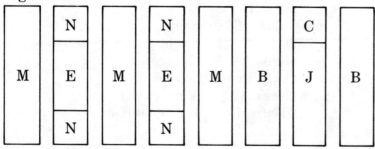

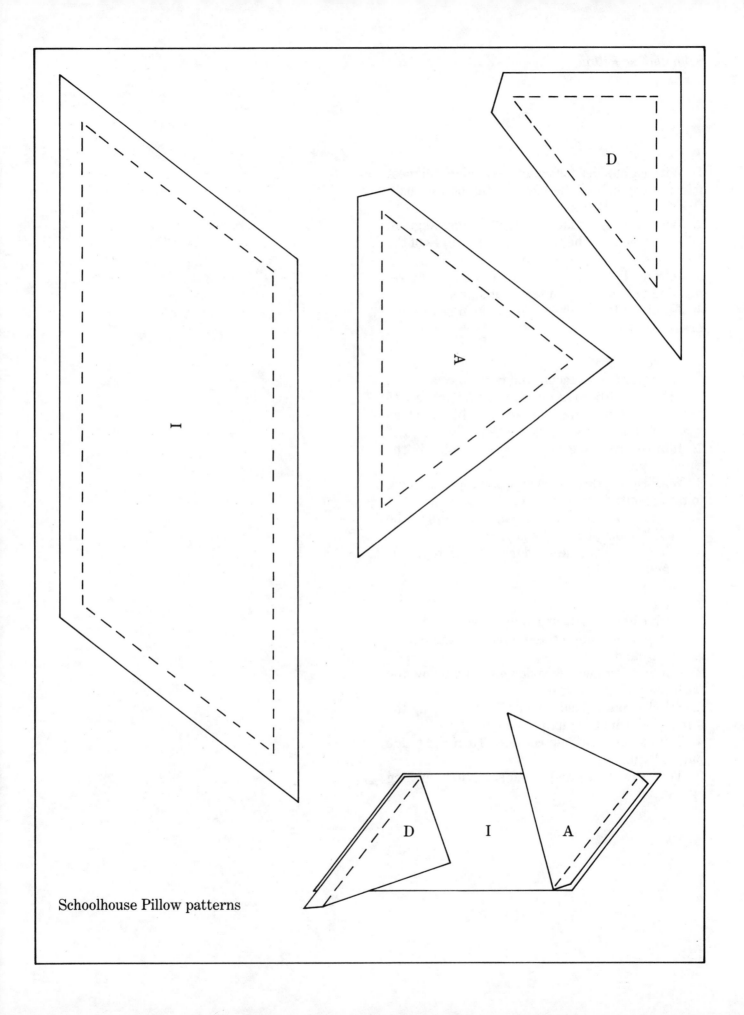

Schoolhouse Pillow patterns

To assemble

1. With right sides facing and raw edges aligned, join the top half of the block to the bottom half. Open seam and press.
2. With right sides facing and raw edges aligned, join an O piece to the top and bottom edges of the house block. Open seams and press.
3. Join an L piece to each short end of the remaining O pieces. Open seams and press.
4. Join to sides of house block. Open seams and press (see Figure 3).

To make borders

1. With right sides facing and raw edges aligned, join short red border pieces (1 × 11 inches) to the top and bottom edges of the block. Open seams and press.
2. Join the red long borders to the sides in the same way.
3. With right sides facing and raw edges aligned, join the white border pieces in the same way.
4. Next, join the navy blue calico borders to the top and bottom and side edges.
5. Join the navy blue border strips to top, bottom, and side edges.

To finish

1. With right sides facing and raw edges aligned, pin the piping around the top piece of the pillow. Stitch around.
2. Pin backing piece face down on the pillow top with the piping between.
3. Stitch around 3 sides and 4 corners, using the stitch line from the piping as a guide.
4. Trim seams and clip corners. Turn right-side out and stuff.
5. Turn raw edges under and slip-stitch opening closed.

Patchwork Tote

Everyone has a variety of small fabric scraps and this is the perfect way to use them. A tote bag made from 1-inch squares is both practical and handsome. This one is done in fall colors, but you might like to use a combination of 2 colors, such as red and white or blue and white, as early quilt makers often did for a bold effect. The strap, back, and lining are made from one of the calico prints. The finished bag is 13½ inches square.

Materials
scraps of calico
⅔ yard brown calico for back, straps, and lining
thin quilt batting

Directions
All fabric measurements for cutting include ¼-inch seam allowance.

Cut the following:
A variety of dark calicos and solids
221 squares 1½ × 1½ inches
Dark calico
    2 pieces 3½ × 33½ inches for straps
    1 piece 14 × 14 inches for back
    2 pieces 14 × 14 inches for lining

To make rows
1. With right sides facing and raw edges aligned, join 3 squares together to make the first row (see diagram).
2. Follow the diagram to make 19 rows of squares. Open all seams and press.
3. With right sides facing and raw edges aligned, join a square to the center square of Row 1 and another square to the center square of Row 19 as shown in diagram.

Joining rows
1. With right sides facing and raw edges aligned, join Row 1 to Row 2 as shown in the diagram.
2. Continue joining all 19 rows in this way. Open seams and press.

To make bag

1. From the patchwork fabric that you have just completed, cut a 14 × 14-inch square on the diagonal as shown by the dotted lines in the diagram.

2. With right sides facing and raw edges aligned, stitch the front and back of the tote bag together around the sides and bottom, leaving the top edge open.

3. Trim seams and clip corners. Turn right-side out.

Lining

1. Cut 2 pieces of quilt batting slightly smaller all around than the lining pieces.

2. Place a piece of batting on the wrong side of the front and back lining pieces and, with right sides of fabric facing, pin all 4 layers together.

3. Stitch around sides and bottom edges, just barely catching the batting at the seam line.

4. Trim seams and clip corners. Do not turn.

5. Slip the lining inside the patchwork tote and line up side and bottom seams.

Handle

1. With right sides facing and raw edges aligned, fold the long fabric strips in half lengthwise. Press.

2. Stitch along one long edge, using ¼-inch seam allowance.

3. Turn right-side out and press. Stitch along the outside edges on right side of fabric. Repeat steps 1 through 3 for second strip.

To finish

1. Turn raw edges around the top of tote and lining ¼ inch to the inside and press.

2. Fold each handle strip in half lengthwise. Measure 3 inches in from the side seams and pin each end of one handle between the outside and lining of the front of the tote.

3. Repeat on the back.

4. Machine-stitch around the top edge of bag.

"14"

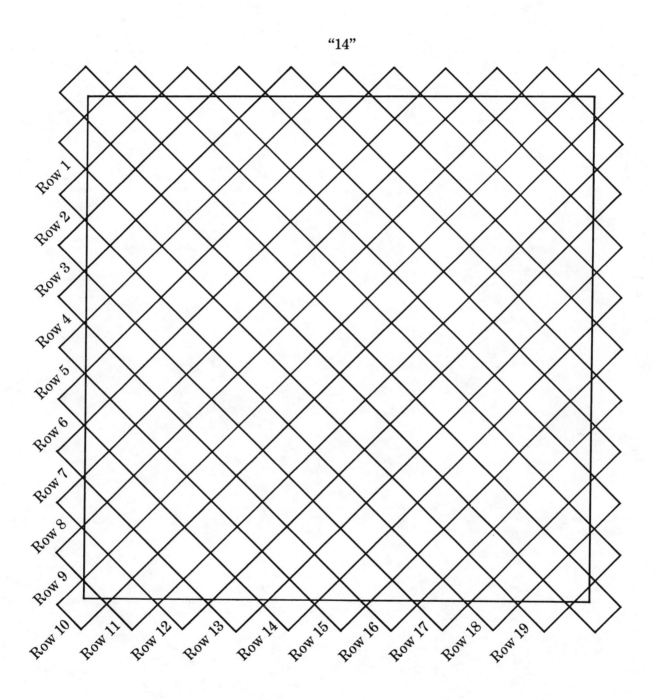

Row 1
Row 2
Row 3
Row 4
Row 5
Row 6
Row 7
Row 8
Row 9
Row 10 Row 11 Row 12 Row 13 Row 14 Row 15 Row 16 Row 17 Row 18 Row 19

For Christmas

Noel Banner

Decorate your front door or entrance hallway for the holidays with this colorful Christmas banner. It's easy to make the appliqués with fusible webbing, calico, and iron-on felt. No stitching required! The finished banner is 22 by 24 inches.

Materials
¼ yard green calico
⅔ yard white Christmas calico
1 yard red calico for backing
small amount of blue calico
small piece each of red and green iron-on felt, or regular felt used with fusible webbing
fusible webbing
1 yard thin quilt batting
tracing paper
stiff paper for template
ballpoint pen
Velcro tabs for hanging

Directions
The pattern pieces for this project are given full size; therefore no enlarging is necessary. Because the appliqués are fused to the fabric background there is no seam allowance.
1. Begin by tracing and transferring the pattern pieces to stiff paper (see page 13).
2. Place each letter template on red felt and draw around the outline with a ballpoint pen.
3. Trace around the circle template to make 3 berries.
4. Using holly pattern piece A on green calico, draw around outline to make 3.
5. Using holly pattern piece B on green felt, draw around outline to make 3.
6. Place the bow pattern on the fold of the blue calico fabric where indicated on the pattern. Pin and trace around template.
7. Pin all fabric pieces, except fusible felt if used, to fusible webbing.

To cut
1. Cut out all appliqué pieces, keeping them pinned to the fusible webbing.
2. Cut white Christmas calico 19½ × 21½ inches.

Figure 1

3. Cut 2 strips of green calico 2 × 21½ inches. Cut 2 strips of green calico 2 × 19½ inches.
4. Cut 4 red calico squares 2 × 2 inches.
5. Cut quilt batting 21½ × 23½ inches.
6. Cut backing fabric 22½ × 24¼ inches.

To assemble
1. Arrange all appliqué pieces in position on the white fabric as shown in Figure 1.
2. Fuse each piece in position, using a medium-hot iron and following directions on the package.
3. With right sides facing and raw edges aligned, join a long green calico strip to the top and bottom edges of the white calico piece. Open seams and press.

4. With right sides facing and raw edges aligned, join a red calico square to each short end of the remaining calico strips. Open seams and press.
5. With right sides facing and raw edges aligned, join these strips to each side of the white fabric top. Open seams and press.

To finish
1. With wrong sides facing, pin the top fabric to the backing with the batting between.
2. Machine-stitch along seam lines of the border through all 3 layers.
3. Turn all raw edges under to inside ¼ inch and press. Slip-stitch all around to finish edges.
4. Hang with Velcro tabs.

Noel Banner letters

Noel Banner

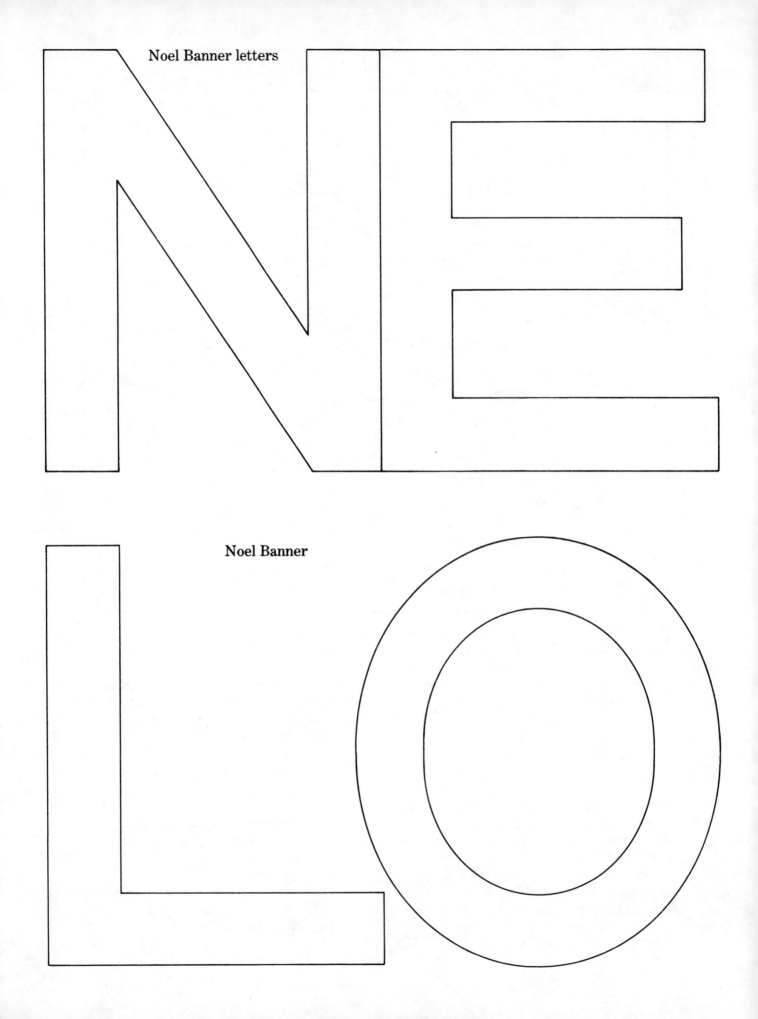

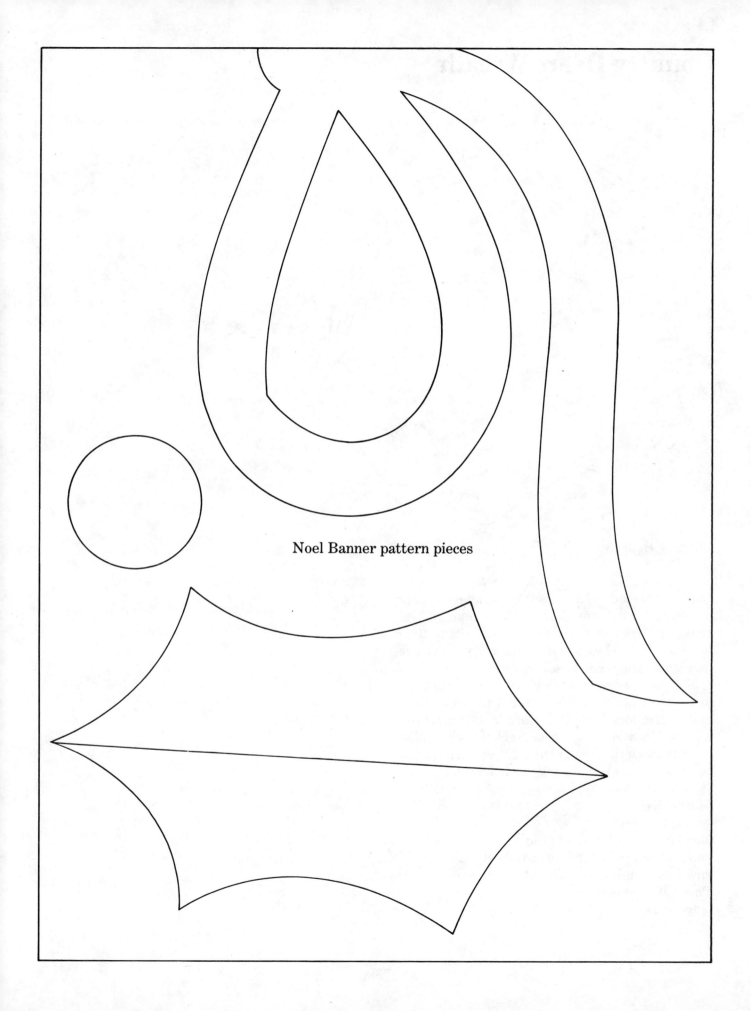

Noel Banner pattern pieces

Country Heart Wreath

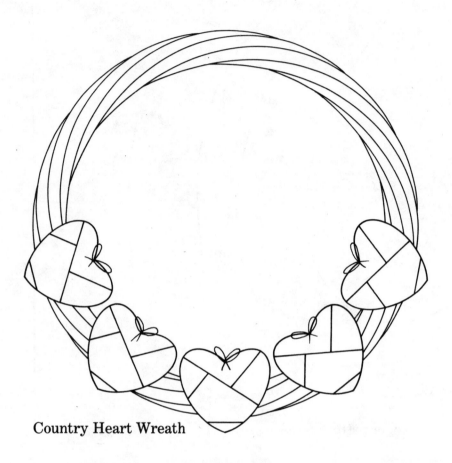

Country Heart Wreath

Wreaths made of honeysuckle, grapevines, and other natural materials provide a country welcome at Christmastime. Some people hang them all year long. They are easy to find at most garden shops and come in several sizes.

The patchwork hearts add a personal touch and are lots of fun to make. Make 5 for the wreath and more for delightful Christmas tree ornaments. They are also good sachets when filled with potpourri. This is the perfect small gift to bring when visiting during the holidays.

Materials
grapevine wreath
small amount of green fabric
small amounts of 4 different red calicos
small amount of white Christmas calico
Poly-Fil™ stuffing
tracing paper
stiff paper

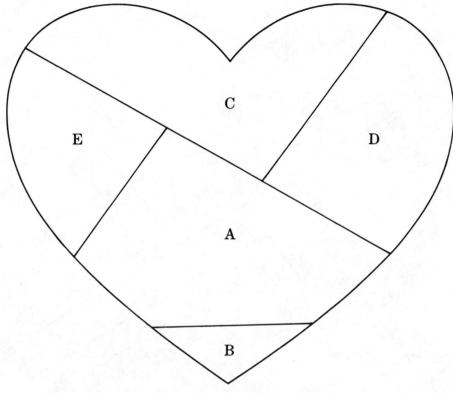

Figure 1

Directions
All patterns include a ¼-inch seam allowance.
1. Trace heart pattern and pieces and transfer to stiff paper for templates (see page 14).
2. Cut 5 different red calico hearts for backings.
3. Cut 5 A pieces out of the green fabric.
4. Cut 5 B, C, D, and E pieces out of different red and white calicos, so you have a variety of pieces.
5. Arrange pattern pieces to make up 5 hearts (see Figure 1).
6. With right sides facing and raw edges aligned, stitch all A pieces to all B pieces. Open seams and press.
7. With right sides facing and raw edges aligned, stitch all C pieces to all D pieces. Join all E pieces to A as shown in Figure 1. Open seams and press.
8. Join sections C-D to sections B-A-E. Open seams and press. You will have 5 crazy-quilt

133

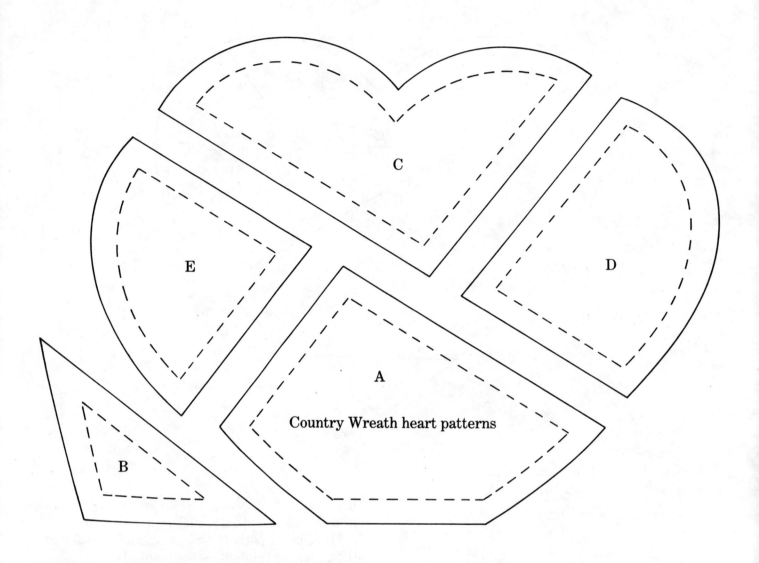

Country Wreath heart patterns

patchwork hearts. If desired, you can add decorative cross-stitch along all joining seams of patchwork to give each heart a country look (see page 22).

9. With right sides facing and raw edges aligned, pin each patchwork heart to backing. Stitch around all hearts, leaving a small opening for turning and stuffing.

10. Trim around seams and turn hearts right-side out.

11. Stuff hearts tightly, turn raw edges under, and slip-stitch opening closed.

12. Arrange stuffed hearts on wreath and tack in position. Decorate wreath with red ribbons, small ornaments, and pinecones, if desired.

Braided Wreath

It takes 3 long strips of red, green, and white Christmas calico to make this braided wreath. Add a big red bow, some pinecones, bells, ribbons, or tiny balls for a festive door decoration.

A creative use for this project is as a punch bowl holder. Make the wreath to fit the diameter of your punch bowl. Place the wreath on a table with the bow in front and set the punch bowl in the center.

The directions for the Santa beanbag are given on page 170.

Materials
¼ yard red calico
¼ yard solid green
¼ yard white Christmas calico
Poly-Fil™ stuffing
4-inch-wide red ribbon for bow
decorations such as pinecones, tiny balls, ribbons, bells, etc.

Directions
All measurements for cutting fabric include a ¼-inch seam allowance.

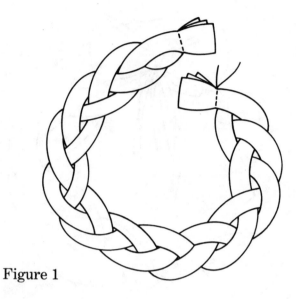

Figure 1

Cut the following:
red calico
   1 strip 6 × 45 inches
green calico
   1 strip 6 × 45 inches
white calico
   1 strip 6 × 45 inches

1. With right sides facing and raw edges aligned, fold each strip in half lengthwise and press.
2. Stitch along the long edge and across one end.
3. Trim seam and turn right-side out.
4. Stuff each tube firmly with stuffing.
5. Pin the open ends of all 3 tubes together.
6. Braid the tubes together and form the braid into a circle. Stitch the ends together (see Figure 1).
7. Turn the wreath so that the stitched ends are at the top.
8. Make a fat bow with the wide ribbon and secure it over the joined ends. Add decorations all around if desired.
9. If you are making this project as a punch bowl holder, the joined ends with the ribbon bow should be in front and the ends of the ribbon spread on the table or hanging over the front of the buffet.

Cookie Cutter Ornaments

These cookie cutter ornaments can be made with all the leftover scraps of colorful fabric from your other projects. Scraps of patchwork fabric from the teddy bear on page 94 are also used for some of the ornaments, adding real country charm to your tree. Or create a tabletop arrangement using a variety of shapes and fabrics, as I've done here.

Materials
scraps of calico
fusible webbing
tracing paper
stiff paper
green, red, or gold cord for hanging

Directions
1. Trace and transfer all shapes to stiff paper.
2. Trace all pattern pieces for the individual ornaments from these pages.
3. Pin each pattern piece to a scrap of fabric on top of a piece of fusible webbing. Cut out each piece.
4. Position each pattern piece of fabric and fusible webbing on the cardboard ornament and fuse with a medium-hot iron.

To finish
1. To add details such as the buttons on the gingerbread man, cut small circles of felt or use tiny buttons and glue in position.
2. You can glue rickrack around the hearts if desired, or add lace, ribbon, eyelet, etc.
3. Poke a hole near the top of each ornament and thread cord through each. Tie to make a hanging loop.
4. The back of each ornament can be finished as you did the front, or you can simply cut a solid piece of fabric, using the shape as a pattern. Fuse to the back as you did the front pieces.

Cookie Cutter Ornament patterns

Cookie Cutter Ornament patterns

Patchwork Heart Pillows

Get out your scraps of fabric for this project. The heart pillow, which is approximately 11 by 13 inches, is the perfect small gift or accent on a bed and will add a bit of holiday cheer to any room. Here are 2 different versions, both created by Susan Joyce. One is made with traditional Christmas calicos, the other with soft pastel green, to match the country stocking.

Materials
a variety of fabrics to make 21-inch-long strips
40 inches of piping
12 × 14-inch piece of backing fabric
Poly-Fil™ stuffing
tracing paper

Directions
All patterns include ¼-inch seam allowance.
1. Enlarge patterns (see page 13).
2. Put the 2 pattern pieces together to form a full heart and trace around it on the wrong side of the backing fabric. Cut out.
3. Cut strips of fabric in varying widths from 1 to 2½ inches and 21 inches long. (These measurements include ¼-inch seam allowance.)
4. With right sides facing and raw edges aligned, join 2 strips along one long edge. Open seams and press.
5. Continue joining strips in this way until you have a piece of fabric measuring 18 × 21 inches.
6. Place pattern pieces A and B on the pieced fabric as shown in Figure 1. The stripes will be going in 2 different directions. Cut out.
7. With right sides facing and raw edges aligned, pin piece A to piece B along split line (as shown in Figure 2) and stitch. Open seams and press.
8. With right sides facing and raw edges aligned, pin the piping to front of pillow all around. Stitch together.
9. With right sides facing and raw edges aligned, pin pillow top to backing. Stitch around, leaving 3 or 4 inches open on one long edge for turning.
10. Trim seams and clip around curves. Turn right-side out and stuff until full.
11. Turn raw edges under ¼ inch and slip-stitch closed.

140

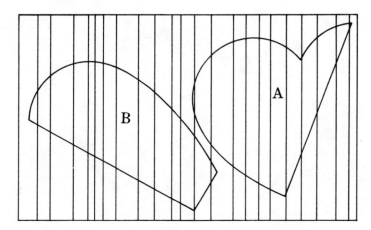

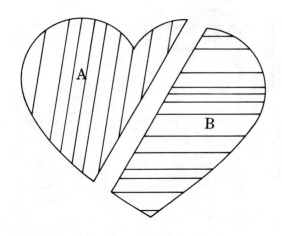

Figure 1 Pattern layout

Figure 2 Heart assembly

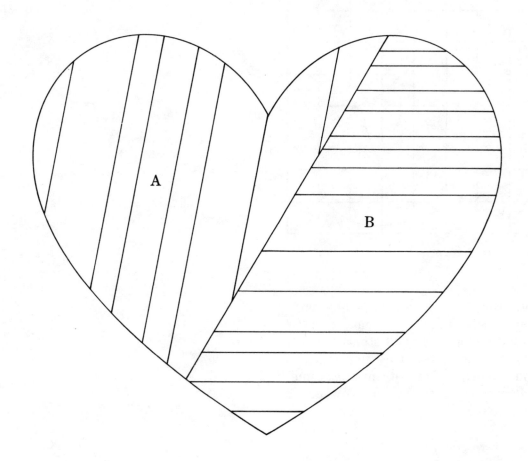

Elf Stocking

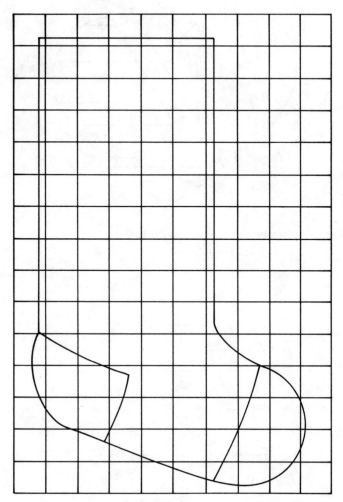

Each square equals 1 inch

This elf stocking is made with a pointed cuff, patch heel, and toe of felt. It's as easy as 1-2-3 with iron-on felt and a bright Christmas print. If you can't find the iron-on felt, most five-and-tens carry red and green felt pieces at Christmastime. Since the felt doesn't fray, no seam allowance is needed when cutting out pattern pieces.

Materials
½ yard red Christmas calico
14 × 18-inch piece of green felt
8 large bells
tracing paper
6 inches of satin or grosgrain ribbon

142

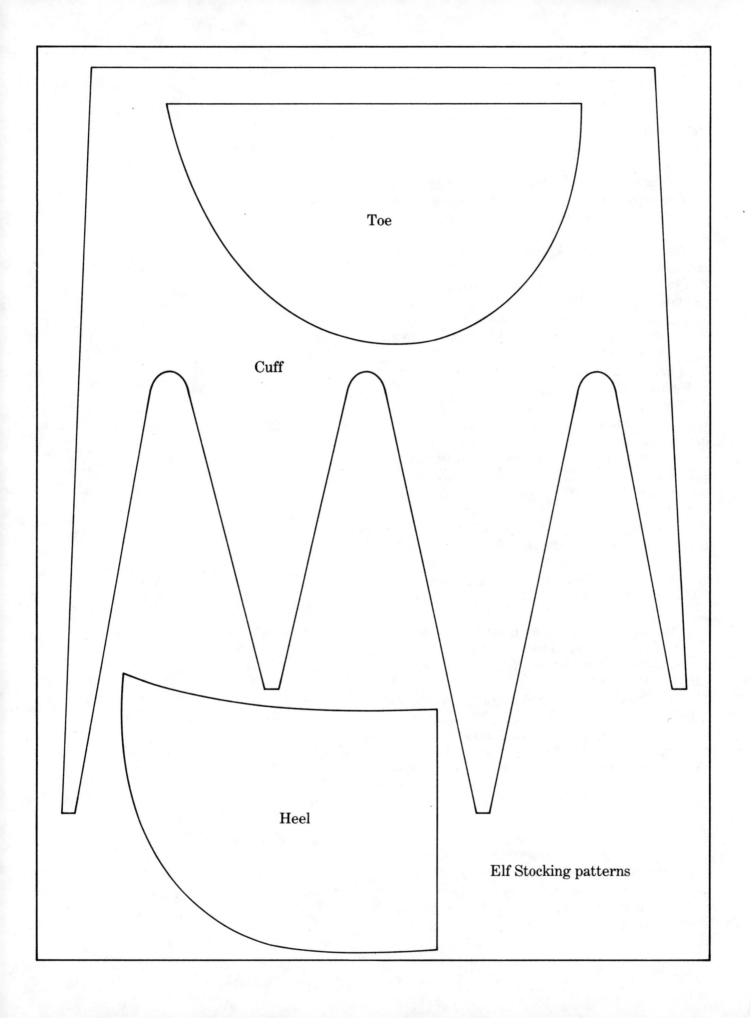

Toe

Cuff

Heel

Elf Stocking patterns

Directions

The stocking is 15 inches long. Each square on the grid equals 1 inch.

1. Enlarge and transfer the pattern to a piece of tracing paper (see page 13). If your tracing paper is smaller than 15 inches long, tape 2 pieces together.

2. Trace the cuff, heel, and toe patterns, which are shown full size.

3. Pin the stocking pattern to a double layer of red fabric and cut out with a ¼-inch seam allowance all around.

4. Cut 2 pieces of felt for the cuff, 2 heels, and 2 toes; no seam allowance needed.

5. If using iron-on felt, cut 2 cuff pieces from the red calico for the cuff lining.

6. With wrong sides facing and all raw edges aligned, fuse the cuff lining to the felt cuff pieces using a medium-hot iron.

7. Pin the heel and toe in position on the front and back pieces of the stocking as indicated on the pattern. Fuse in place with a medium-hot iron. If using regular felt, stitch along only the straight edge of the heel and toe pieces.

8. With right sides facing and raw edges aligned, pin the front and back of the stocking together and stitch along the edges, leaving the top edge open. Trim seams as close to the stitching as possible.

9. With right sides facing and raw edges aligned, pin the front and back of the cuff pieces together. Stitch along each side seam. Trim seams. Do not turn to right side.

10. Slip the cuff inside the stocking and line up side seams and top raw edges. Pin and stitch around top edge with a ¼-inch seam allowance.

11. Turn cuff to the right side of stocking and press. Stitch around the top front edge of the cuff, as close to the top edge as possible for a neat finish.

To finish

You might want to add a ribbon or decorative trim around the top edge, and you can tack a bell to the end of each point of the cuff. Fold the 6-inch ribbon in half lengthwise and tack inside top seam for hanging.

Pastel Lacy Stocking

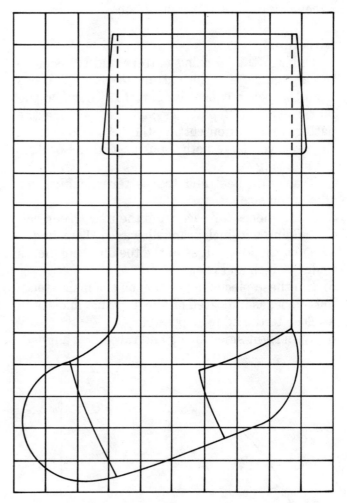

Each square equals 1 inch

Who can resist a delicate, lacy, pastel Christmas stocking? Make this one for a favorite teen, sister, mother, aunt. The color combination is up to you, but keep it light. The overall white print on a background color is especially pretty. Add ribbon and eyelet to satin or delicate calico fabric for a full cuff, and create a soft country scene with fabric-wrapped gifts.

Materials
½ yard peach calico
¼ yard mint green calico
16 inches of 3-inch-wide white eyelet
16 inches of 2-inch-wide peach-colored ribbon
tracing paper

6 inches ½-inch-wide satin ribbon

Directions
1. Enlarge the stocking pattern and transfer to tracing paper. Use this pattern to cut out 2 pieces from the peach calico. Be sure to either fold the fabric and cut 2 patterns at once, or turn the pattern over when cutting the second piece. In this way you have both the front and the back of the stocking.
2. Trace the heel and toe patterns, which are shown full size.
3. Cut 2 pieces for each from the mint green calico, adding a ¼-inch seam allowance all around.
4. Turn the long edges of the toe and heel pieces under ¼ inch and press.
5. Pin these pieces in position on the main stocking fabric, as indicated on the drawing, and stitch as close to the edge as possible.
6. With right sides facing and raw edges aligned,

Pastel Lacy Stocking patterns

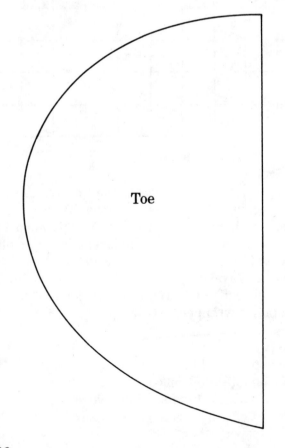

Toe

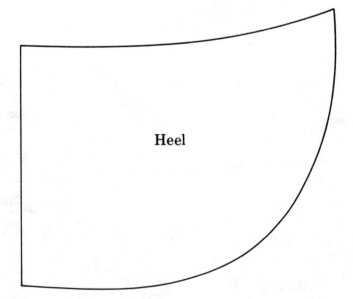

Heel

join the front and back of the stocking together by stitching around with a ¼-inch seam allowance. Leave the top edge open.

7. Trim seams all around and clip around curves. Turn right-side out. Press.

To make cuff

1. Enlarge and transfer cuff pattern to tracing paper (see page 13).

2. Use this pattern to cut 4 pieces of fabric for outside and lining of the cuff.

3. With right sides facing and raw edges aligned, stitch 2 cuff pieces together along the short ends. Repeat with the remaining cuff pieces. Open seams and press. Do not turn.

4. Slip one cuff inside the other and align seams and top raw edges. Pin around top and bottom edges. Stitch around bottom edge only. Trim seam.

5. Turn right-side out and press.

6. With right sides facing and raw edges aligned, stitch eyelet together along short ends. Turn right-side out.

7. Slip eyelet cuff over fabric cuff so top edges match. Stay-stitch around top edge.

8. With right sides facing, join short ends of 2-inch-wide ribbon. Pin around top edge of cuff and stay-stitch.

9. Fold ½-inch-wide ribbon in half lengthwise. With raw edges aligned and loop inside stocking, pin at side seam.

10. Slip the entire cuff inside stocking and pin around top raw edge. Stitch around, leaving a ¼-inch seam allowance.

11. Trim seam and turn cuff right-side out. Stitch around outside top edge of cuff for neat finish.

For Bazaars

Scented Fabric Hangers

It's easy to cover wooden hangers with your choice of fabrics for an elegant gift or to pretty up your closets. These padded hangers have a patchwork heart sachet hanging from each to give your clothes and closet a sweet scent.

Materials

wooden coat hangers
piece of fabric 3 inches wide and longer than hanger by 5 inches (see Figure 1)
quilt batting same size as fabric
scraps of calico for sachet
12 inches 1-inch eyelet for each sachet
12 inches ½-inch satin ribbon for each sachet
handful of potpourri for each sachet
Poly-Fil™ stuffing

Directions

1. Fold one long edge of the fabric under ¼ inch and press.
2. Wrap the quilt batting around the wooden hanger so it is evenly padded and not too tight. There will be 1½ inches of padding extending on each end (see Figure 2).
3. Take large, loose basting stitches across the batting to hold it in place.
4. Place the padded hanger on top of the wrong side of the fabric, with the raw edge of fabric at the top.
5. Make a slit in the fabric for the hook. Wrap the fabric around the batting so that the bottom, turned edge fits over the raw edge at the top. Slit the fabric to fit the hook and turn the slit edges under.
6. Secure edges around hook with a slip stitch, drawing them together. Slip-stitch along top fabric edge (see Figure 3).
7. Take a small running stitch around each end of the hanger and pull to gather the fabric loosely. Tuck excess fabric ends inside and pull stitches tight to close.

To make sachets
1. Trace the heart pattern and use each section to cut a fabric piece, adding a ¼-inch seam allowance.

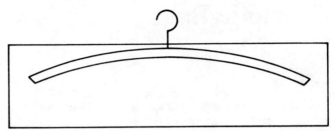

Figure 1   Cut fabric 5 inches wide and 3 inches
             longer than hanger.

Fold.

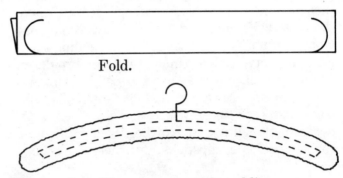

Figure 2   Wrap hanger with padding.

Figure 3   Stitch opening closed.

2. Follow Figure 1 and piece together. Use the pieced heart pattern to cut a solid piece for the backing.

3. With right sides facing and raw edges aligned, stitch the eyelet to the patchwork front of the heart.

4. With right sides facing and raw edges aligned, stitch backing to the front of the heart, leaving a small opening for turning and stuffing.

5. Put a small amount of stuffing into the bottom half of the heart and fill the rest with potpourri.

6. Stitch opening closed with a slip stitch. Add a ribbon bow to the top of the heart and tack the sachet in place on the hanger.

Cosmetic Bags

Before I ever began crafting, my grandmother used to send me little cosmetic bags. I used them for everything and over the years had quite a collection, made from various scraps of fabrics left over from her many crafting projects. Nanna turned ninety-eight this year and doesn't make the little bags anymore, but I always remember what useful gifts they were, so I am adding them here in pretty calico trimmed with embroidered ribbons. Each one matches the padded hangers and is lined with a contrasting fabric. The finished size is 5½ by 6½ inches. They make wonderful little gifts that can be filled with guest soaps, perfume, lipsticks, brushes, or a lacy hanky.

Materials
piece of light calico 12 × 13½ inches
piece of dark calico 12 × 13½ inches
decorative embroidered ribbon 2 × 7 inches
thin quilt batting 6½ × 11 inches
7-inch zipper in color to match fabric

Directions
1. Cut each fabric piece in half lengthwise so you have 2 pieces 6 × 13½ inches. One is the outside and the other the lining.
2. Turn the short, raw edges under ¼ inch and press.
3. Pin the ribbon to the top edge of the front of the outside fabric, ⅛ inch from the folded edge.
4. With right sides facing and raw edges aligned, fold each piece of fabric in half lengthwise and pin along side edges. Stitch.
5. Turn the outside fabric right-side out. Do not turn the lining piece.
6. Fold the batting piece in half lengthwise and slip inside bag. Slip the lining in and smooth in position so side seams line up and top edges are even.
7. Slip-stitch top edges together. Set zipper in top and stitch in position as directed on package.

Lined Baskets

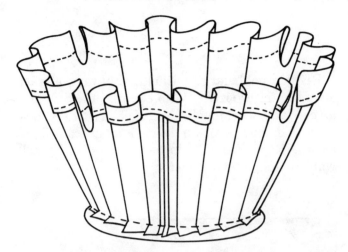

Any purchased basket can be lined with pretty fabrics and used to hold food, potpourri, soaps, or plants. This is a nice way to turn an ordinary item into something special. They make terrific bazaar items and create a colorful area for displaying your goods.

Materials
fabric 3 inches wider than depth of basket and
    long enough to wrap around twice
1 package of bias binding
3-inch-wide ribbon to make a fat bow

Directions
1. Place the basket on the fabric and draw around the base. Cut out.
2. For sloping baskets as shown here, measure 1½ times around the basket at the widest part and measure the depth. Add 2½ inches to this measurement. Cut a rectangle to these dimensions.
3. With right sides facing, stitch short ends together.
4. Gather the fabric evenly to fit the base and pin with right sides together. Stitch around. Trim seam allowance.
5. If the basket has handles, cut and bias-bind slits to fit them. Leave enough on either end to tie into bows.
6. Turn top raw edge of fabric to wrong side to make a 1-inch hem.
7. Fit lining into basket and turn hem over the rim to the outside.
8. Slip-stitch bias binding to outside edge. Add a big bow to the front of the fabric hem.

Patchwork Potholders

Bright, bold, large potholders always attract attention at a bazaar. Who can resist a new and attractive potholder? These reflect a country look with their patchwork quilt designs in traditional colors. Each one is 8 inches square and you'll want to keep one or two for yourself.

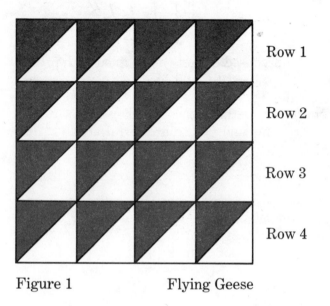

Figure 1   Flying Geese

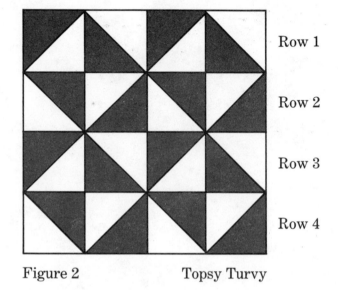

Figure 2   Topsy Turvy

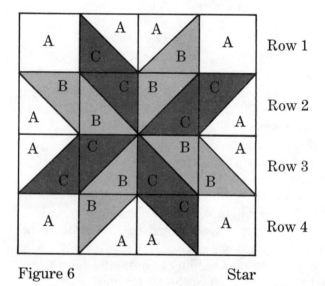

Figure 6   Star

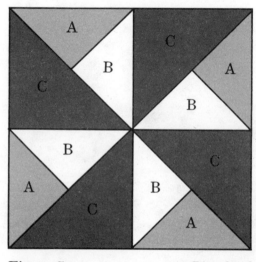

Figure 5   Pinwheel

Materials (to make 4)
¼ yard red calico
¼ yard blue calico
¼ yard white solid fabric
16 × 16 inches thin quilt batting for each potholder

Directions

Flying Geese

For this pattern you will use the quick and easy triangle method of stitching the pieces together (see page 19). In this way you can make any of the patterns in no time at all, which makes this project especially good for a bazaar item or quick gift.

1. Measure and mark 8 squares 3 × 3 inches on the white fabric.
2. Draw a diagonal line in the same direction through all the marked squares.
3. With right sides facing and raw edges aligned, pin the marked white fabric to the red calico fabric.
4. Stitch ¼ inch on both sides of the diagonal lines.
5. Cut on all solid lines. Open seams and press.

To make a row

1. Join 4 squares together, making sure the triangle colors are all in the same position (i.e., all white triangles on the left, red on right).
2. Make 4 rows in this way as shown in Figure 1. Open seams and press.
3. With right sides facing and raw edges aligned, join Row 1 to Row 2. Continue to join all 4 rows in this way. Open seams and press.

Quilting

1. Cut 2 pieces of batting 8 × 8 inches for each potholder.
2. Pin top of potholder to the 2 layers of batting and machine-quilt ¼ inch on both sides of all seam lines. Remove pins.

To finish

1. Cut the red calico backing piece 9 × 9 inches.

2. With *wrong* sides facing, pin quilted top and backing piece together with the batting between. There will be ½ inch of backing fabric all around.

3. Fold raw edge of backing ¼ inch to wrong side of fabric and press.

4. Bring the backing edges over to the front of the top to create a narrow, ¼-inch border all around.

5. Press and machine- or slip-stitch all around.

6. Make a hanging loop from the red calico and attach to the back of one corner.

Topsy Turvy

Use the quick and easy triangle method for this project (see page 19).

1. Measure and mark 8 squares 3 × 3 inches on white fabric. Draw a line diagonally through all squares.

2. With right sides facing and raw edges aligned, pin the white fabric to the blue calico.

3. Stitch ¼ inch on each side of the diagonal lines.

4. Cut on all solid lines. Open seams and press.

5. With right sides facing and raw edges aligned, join 4 squares together as shown in Figure 2 to make Row 1 across. Refer to Figure 2 and make all 4 rows.

6. With right sides facing and raw edges aligned, join Row 1 to Row 2. Continue to join all 4 rows in this way. Open seams and press.

7. Quilt and finish as for Flying Geese, using blue calico backing.

Pinwheels

Directions

All measurements for fabric include ¼-inch seam allowance.

Cut the following:
red calico (A)
   2 squares 3⅞ × 3⅞ inches—cut into 2
     triangles each
white (B)
   2 squares 3⅞ × 3⅞ inches—cut into 2
     triangles each

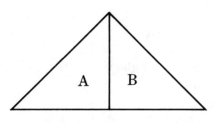

Figure 3

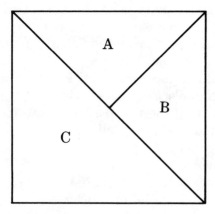

Figure 4

blue calico (C)

    2 squares 5 × 5 inches—cut into 2 triangles each

1. With right sides facing and raw edges aligned, join A triangles to B triangles to make 4 larger triangles (see Figure 3).

2. Join large AB triangle to C triangle along the diagonal to make a square 4½ × 4½ inches (see Figure 4). Make 4. Open seams and press.

3. With right sides facing and raw edges aligned, join the 4 squares together as shown in Figure 5.

4. Quilt and finish as for Flying Geese.

Star

    Use the quick and easy triangle method (see page 19).

1. Measure and mark 2 squares 3 × 3 inches on the white fabric (B). Draw a line diagonally through the squares.

2. With right sides facing and raw edges aligned, pin the marked fabric to a piece of red calico (A) cut to the same size and sew ¼ inch on each side of marked diagonal lines.

3. Cut on solid lines. Open seams and press.

4. Repeat steps 1 through 3 using white (B) with blue calico (C).

5. Repeat steps 1 thorugh 3 using red calico (A) and blue calico (C).

6. Cut 4 squares of white (B) 2½ × 2½ inches.

7. With right sides facing and raw edges aligned, join 4 squares together to make a row, as shown in Figure 6. Continue to make 4 rows this way as shown in Figure 6. Open seams and press.

8. With right sides facing and raw edges aligned, join Row 1 to Row 2. Continue to join all 4 rows in this way. Open seams and press.

9. Quilt and finish as for Flying Geese, using blue calico for backing.

Whimsical Bibs

Use terry cloth and scraps of fabric to make simple appliqué bibs. Each one is trimmed with bias binding and the facial details are hand embroidered. If you make several at one time it is economical and timesaving. The happy animal faces help to create a fanciful and attractive booth for bazaar selling. Or you might like to make one to give as a gift, using colorful scraps that you have left over from another project.

Materials

⅓ yard white terry cloth
scraps of calico
1 skein black embroidery floss for cat and
    bunny bibs
embroidery needle
fusible webbing
1 package double-width bias binding

Directions

1. If you are making the bunny bib, trace the main piece from this book. Then trace the ear pattern and tape in position where indicated on the main pattern piece.
2. Place the pattern on the fold of the terry cloth fabric and cut out.
3. If making the cat or chicken bib, trace the pattern and place on fold of fabric. Cut out.
4. The rest of the pattern pieces are for the appliqués and are shown full size. Trace each piece.
5. Select the colors for each element—eyes, nose, cheeks, ears, chicken, egg, etc.—and pin the correct pattern to the fabric and a piece of fusible webbing. Cut out each piece.
6. Position each appliqué on the terry cloth as shown in the diagrams and fuse with a medium-hot iron.
7. Using your pattern as a guide, draw mouth and whiskers with a light pencil on the terry cloth bib.
8. Using 3 strands of embroidery floss, take small running stitches over the pencil lines.
9. Encase entire edge of bib in bias binding, pin, and slip-stitch all around.
10. Cut 2 lengths of binding or ½-inch ribbon approximately 12 inches long for neck ties, and stitch in position (about 4 inches apart) on the top inside edge of each bib.

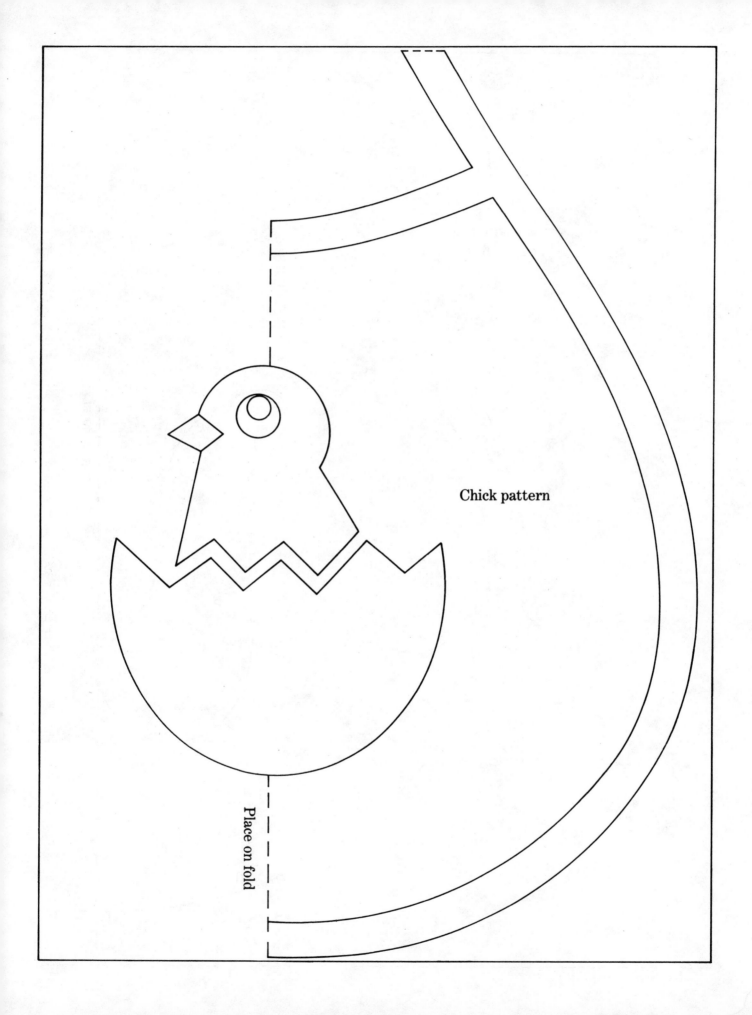

Chick pattern

Place on fold

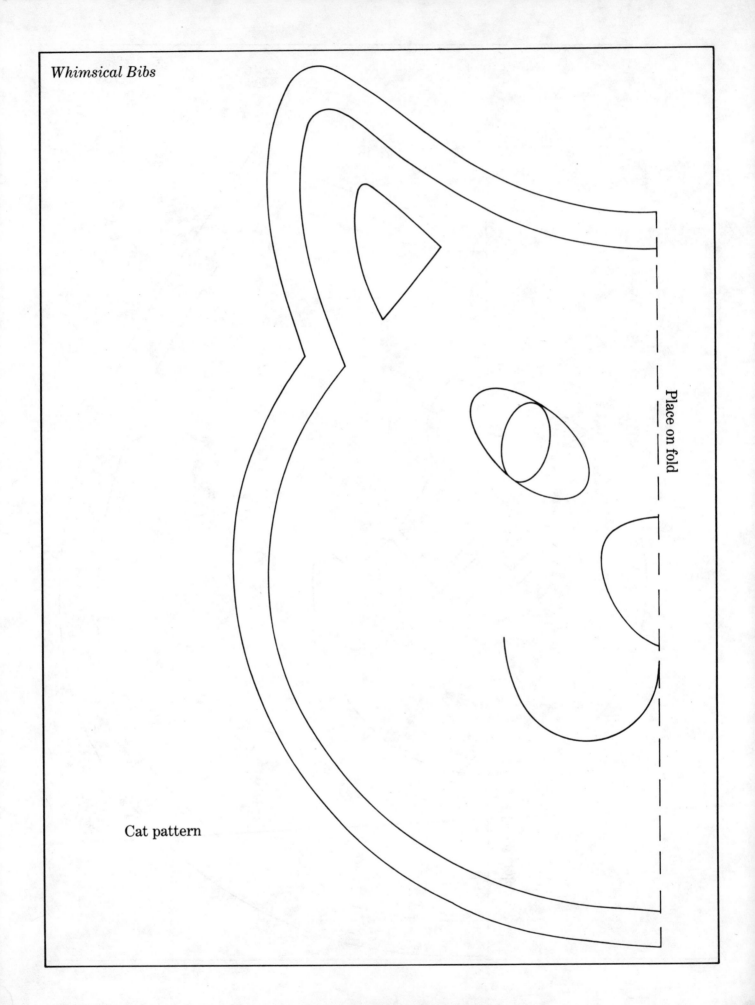

Whimsical Bibs

Place on fold

Cat pattern

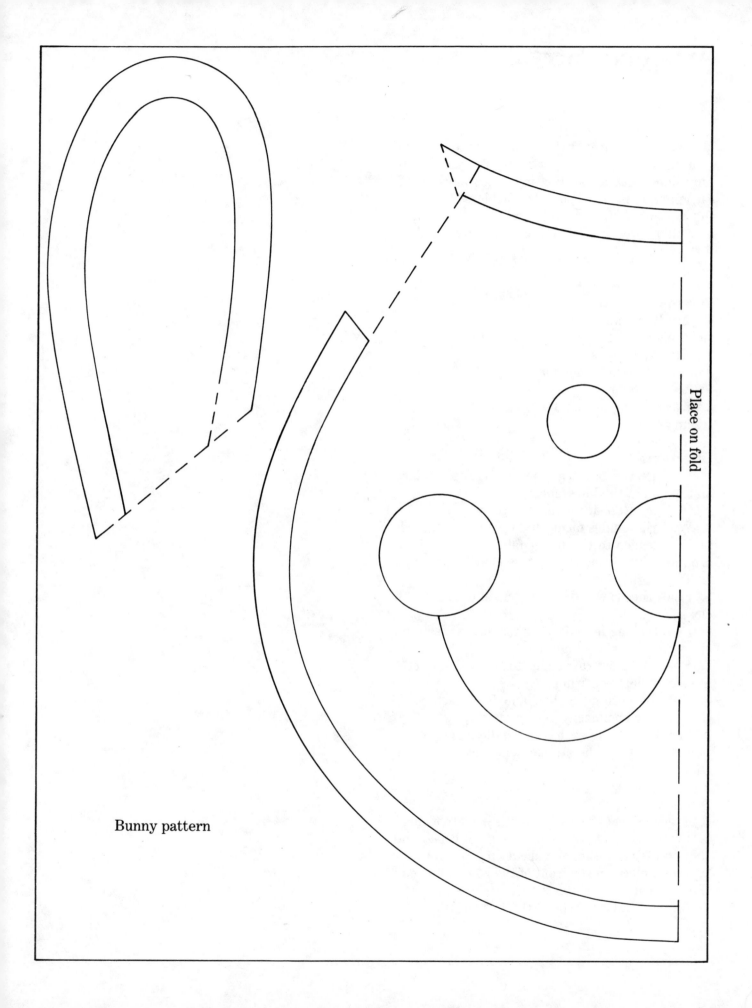

Bunny pattern

Place on fold

Appliqué Carryall

Carry your craftwork in progress or baby's gear in style. This roomy 17 by 20-inch bag is fully lined with a coordinating calico fabric. The cat appliqué is attached with fusible webbing. If the cat isn't your favorite, choose one of the animal pillow designs from page 76, which will fit just as well.

Materials
½ yard blue calico
½ yard lining fabric
small piece of yellow and brown calico
2 buttons (cat eyes)
8 inches of ⅛-inch-wide blue satin ribbon
fusible webbing
2 yards cording for handle
tracing paper

Directions
1. Enlarge the pattern (see page 13) and place on the fold of the blue fabric.
2. Cut out. Repeat for the lining.
3. With right sides facing and raw edges aligned, pin blue calico to the lining fabric and stitch all around, leaving one small edge open for turning.
4. Turn right-side out and press.
5. Fold the raw edges under and slip-stitch closed.
6. Fold the bag in half so the top edges meet and slip-stitch the sides together.
7. Fold the short raw edges to the inside to create a channel for cording.
8. Cut the cording in half and feed each piece through the channels.
9. Sew the ends of each cord handle together and pull it around so the stitched ends are inside the channel.

Appliqué
1. Trace the cat and tail patterns from this book.
2. Pin the cat pattern to the yellow calico and then to fusible webbing and cut out.
3. Pin in place on the front of the bag and fuse to the bag using a medium-hot iron.
4. Pin the tail pattern on the brown calico and

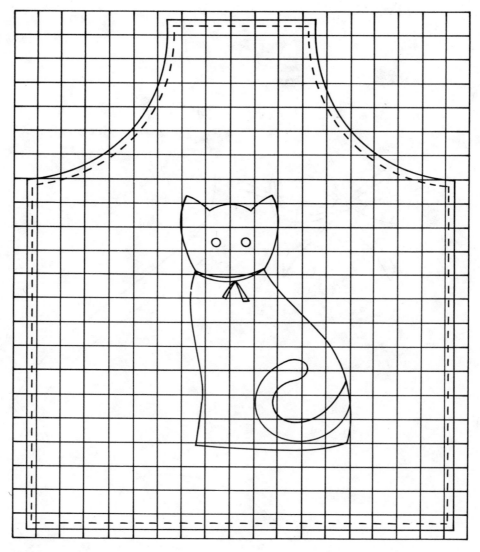

Each square equals 1 inch

then to fusible webbing and cut out.

5. Pin in place on the cat and fuse with iron.

6. Stitch button eyes in place on cat's face.

7. Make a small ribbon bow and glue or stitch at the cat's neck.

Appliqué Carryall

Cat pattern

Beanbags

This is a popular bazaar item for young children as well as teenagers. The frogs have googly eyes and are silly-looking. The octopus is right at home with his "legs" straddling a shelf. Santa is fun all year long, and the juggling balls will delight young and old alike.

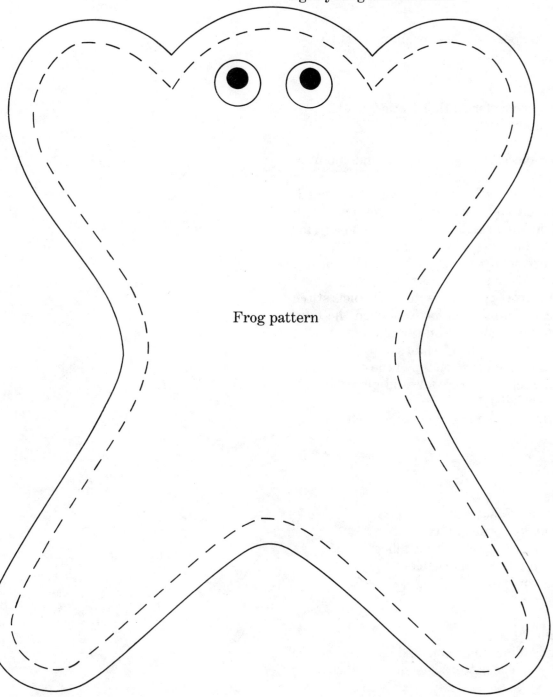

Frog pattern

Frog

Materials
piece of green calico 6 × 8 inches
piece of blue fabric 6 × 8 inches
2 white pom-poms
scrap of black felt
white glue
beans, seeds, peas, or corn for filling
tracing paper

Directions
The pattern piece for cutting fabric includes a ¼-inch seam allowance.
1. Trace the frog pattern from this book.
2. Cut one piece from green fabric and one from the blue.
3. With right sides facing and raw edges aligned, pin the green and blue fabrics together. Stitch around, leaving a small opening at the mouth for turning and filling.
4. Trim around seams and clip around curves. Turn right-side out and press.
5. Fill the frog two-thirds full. Do not stitch opening closed until you have stitched the eyes in place so you can reach in to hold your needle on the underside of the top fabric.
6. Stitch pom-pom eyes on top of the calico head. Cut small circles of black felt and glue them on the white eyeballs.
7. Turn raw edges under and slip-stitch opening closed.

Octopus

Materials
small amount of blue calico
small amount of peach calico
beans, seeds, peas, or corn for filling
2 white pom-poms or moveable eyes
tracing paper
stiff paper

Directions
The body is 9 inches around and each tentacle is 6 inches long. The pattern includes a ¼-inch seam allowance.

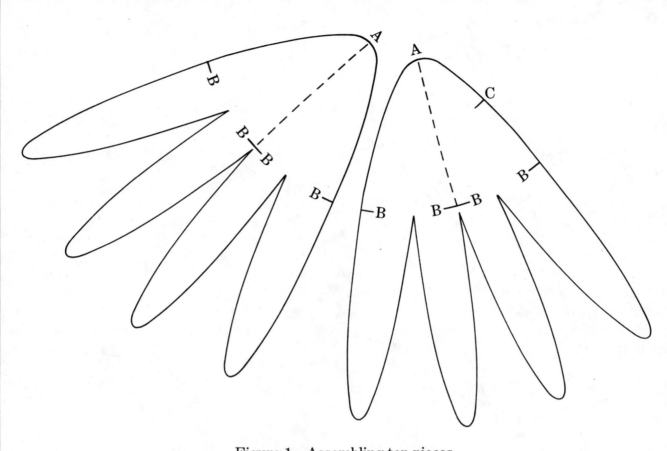

Figure 1   Assembling top pieces

Figure 2   Underbody assembly

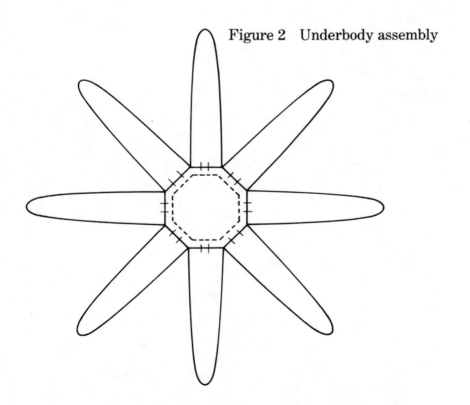

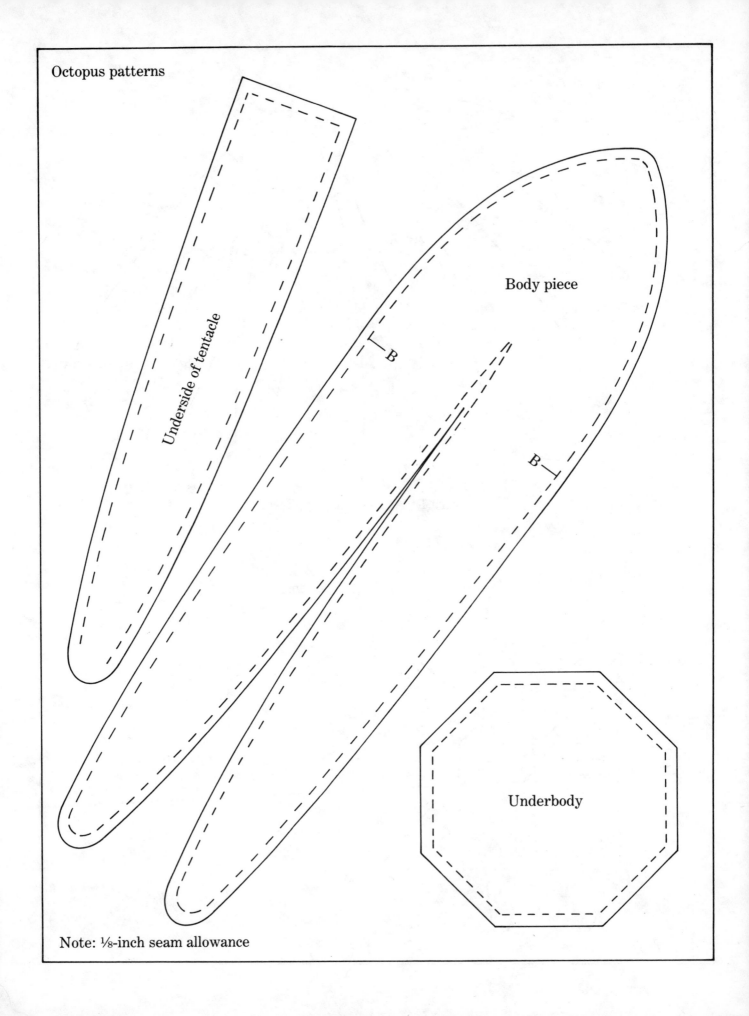

Octopus patterns

Underside of tentacle

Body piece

B

B

Underbody

Note: ⅛-inch seam allowance

1. Trace the patterns and transfer to stiff paper for a template (see page 14).

2. Using the template, draw around the body on the wrong side of the blue calico 4 times.

3. Using the template for the underside of the tentacles, draw 8 on the wrong side of the peach calico.

4. Using the underbody pattern, draw one on the wrong side of the peach calico.

5. Cut out all pieces.

6. With right sides facing and raw edges aligned, pin 2 body pieces together and stitch down one side from point A to point B on broken line, as shown in Figure 1.

7. Repeat with the other 2 body pieces.

8. With right sides facing and raw edges aligned, pin the 2 top pieces together. Stitch from the left-hand point B up over the top past point A to C, leaving an opening from C to the right-hand point B and continuing down to the edge of the tentacle.

Lining

1. With right sides facing and raw edges aligned, pin the 8 peach tentacles to the underbody piece (see Figure 2). Stitch around.

2. With right sides facing and raw edges aligned, pin the underbody and tentacle lining to the head and tentacles, matching the bases of the tentacles. Stitch around all tentacles.

3. Clip curves between tentacles. Cut across the tips of each tentacle close to the seams.

4. Turn the octopus right-side out and fill with beans.

5. Turn raw edges under and slip-stitch opening closed.

6. Stitch 2 pom-pom eyes in place on front of face.

Juggling Balls: 3

Materials
small amounts of red, blue, green, and yellow
   calico
small beans for filling
tracing paper
stiff paper

Directions

This is a very easy project to make from 2 pieces of fabric, one pattern, and a continuous seam. Each ball is 9½ inches around. The pattern includes a ¼-inch seam allowance.

1. Trace the pattern and transfer to stiff paper for a template (see page 13).
2. Place the template on the wrong side of the fabric and draw around once on the red, blue, and green calico. Make 3 on yellow fabric.
3. Cut out all fabric pieces.
4. With right sides facing and raw edges aligned, pin a yellow piece to the red piece, matching the end marks on the yellow with the center marks on the red, and the end marks on the red to the center marks on the yellow.
5. Repeat, using a yellow piece and the blue piece.
6. Repeat, using a yellow piece and the green piece.
7. Stitch a continuous seam all around each ball, leaving a small opening for turning and filling.
8. Turn right-side out and fill with small beans. Turn raw edges under and slip-stitch opening closed.

Santa

Materials

small scraps of red, green, blue, and pink calico
small beans for filling
3 yards white yarn
embroidery needle
2 tiny moveable eyes or black felt
white glue
pom-pom for nose
tracing paper
fusible webbing

Directions

All patterns include a ¼-inch seam allowance. The Santa beanbag is 15 inches tall.

1. Trace the pattern pieces from these pages.
2. Fold the red calico in half and cut out the body and hat.

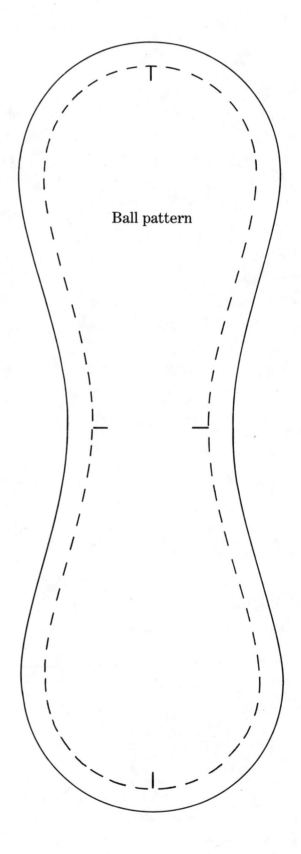

Ball pattern

3. Fold the pink fabric in half and cut out the face pattern.

4. Cut 2 green boots. Turn pattern over and cut 2 more.

5. Cut 2 gloves, toes, and heels from blue fabric. Turn patterns over and cut 2 more of each.

6. With right sides facing and raw edges aligned, stitch the hat pieces to the face pieces along the top edge of the face.

7. Join face pieces to the body pieces at the neck in the same way.

8. Next, join the glove pieces to the arms, and boot pieces to the legs. Open all seams and press.

9. Cut a piece of fusible webbing for the heel and toe pieces and position fabric and webbing on boot. Fuse with a medium-hot iron.

10. With right sides facing and raw edges aligned, pin Santa's front and back together and stitch around, leaving a small opening in the side of the hat for turning and filling.

11. Turn right-side out and fill.

12. Turn raw edges under and slip-stitch opening closed.

To finish

1. Glue moveable eyes in place on face.

2. Stitch nose in center of face.

3. Using the embroidery needle and white yarn, make big loops around face for beard.

4. Add a pom-pom tassel to the top of Santa's hat.

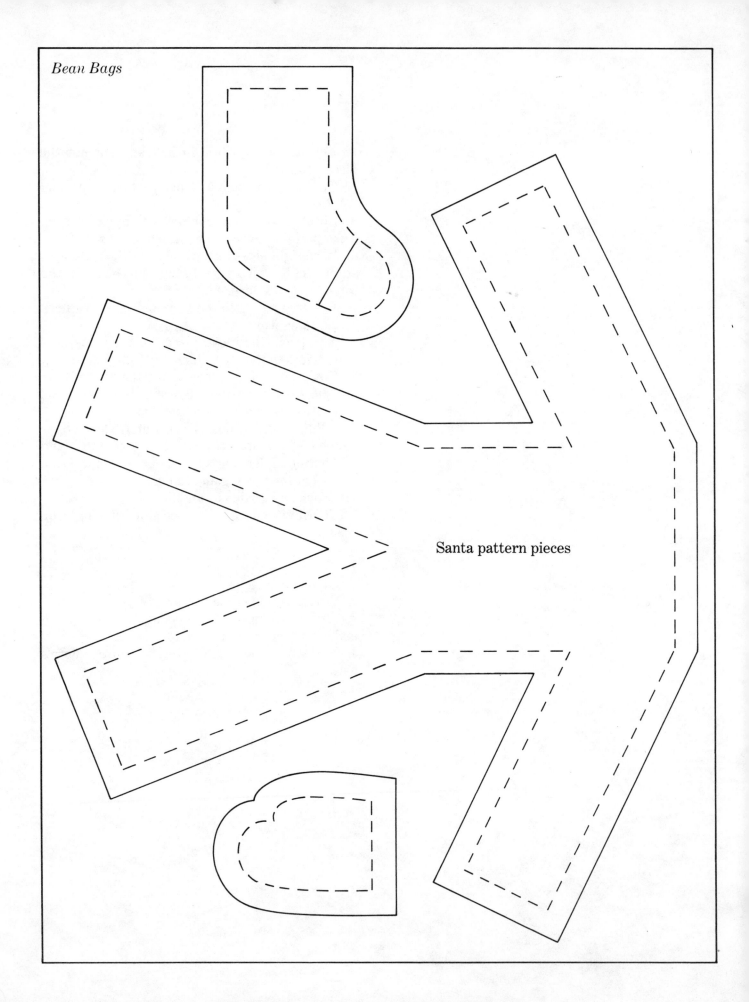

Bean Bags

Santa pattern pieces

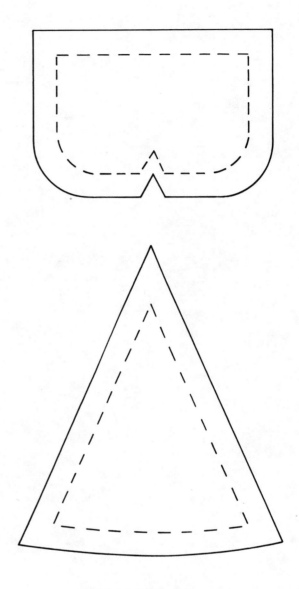

Santa pattern pieces

Sources for Supplies

Fabric

Quilt Patch
261 Main Street
Northboro, MA 01532

If you can't find a good variety of 100 percent cotton fabric, this is the source for all your calicos, as well as solids, ginghams, and polished cottons. They also carry muslin and cotton sheeting at reasonable prices. If you send $3.00 to the above address, you will receive four hundred swatches of fabric and a price list.

The Weston Country Store
Weston, VT 05161

They carry calico fabrics, and if you can't find a specific pattern or have run out of something, you might try this source for your supply.

Potpourri for sachets

Caswell-Massey Co. Ltd.
518 Lexington Avenue
New York, NY 10017

Mail Orders:
111 Eighth Avenue
New York, NY 10011

Quilt supplies

Extra Special Products, Inc.
P.O. Box 777
Greenville, OH 45331

I like the products from this company. They have plastic triangles to make perfect stars, pre-marked rulers for mitering perfect corners, and plastic grids.

Fairfield Processing Corporation
P.O. Box 1157
Danbury, CT 06810

If you do any crafting you've probably used the quilt batting from Fairfield Processing Corp. Poly-Fil™ is the brand name for their quality polyester fiber, which comes in a variety of thicknesses. The quilt batting is packaged in different sizes common to most beds and cribs, but you can also buy it by the yard. All the information is on the package and it is carried wherever fabric and quilt supplies are sold.